The Civil Service Application & Interview Guide

CVs, STAR Examples and Interview Tips for EO, HEO & SEO Roles

Stewart Paterson

© 2025 Stewart Paterson. All rights reserved.

No part of this publication may be reproduced, stored in a retrieval system, or transmitted in any form or by any means — electronic, mechanical, photocopying, recording, or otherwise — without the prior written permission of the author.

This book is intended to provide helpful guidance but does not guarantee any outcome. All views are the author's own.

Contents

Introduction: Why This Guide Exists 1

Chapter 1: The Civil Service Landscape 3

Chapter 2: Demystifying Success Profiles 10

Chapter 3: Writing Your Civil Service CV (Experience Section) 19

Chapter 4: Writing a Strong Personal Statement 28

Chapter 5: How to Write Behaviour Statements That Work 36

Chapter 6: Mastering the Sift Stage 61

Chapter 7: Nailing the Interview Stage 64

Chapter 8: Common Mistakes & Easy Fixes 78

Chapter 9: Templates, Tools & Final Tips 81

Chapter 10: Final Words: Good Luck — What Awaits You 84

Introduction: Why This Guide Exists

So, you're trying to get a job in the Civil Service — maybe for the first time, or maybe after a few frustrating attempts that didn't go your way. Either way, you're in the right place.

This guide exists because the Civil Service application process can feel like a maze. From behaviour statements and sift scores to interviews that seem designed to trip you up, it's easy to get discouraged. And the truth is, a lot of people do. I've seen it firsthand — and I've been there myself.

For a while, I was stuck in a cycle of rejection. I kept applying for Executive Officer (**EO**) roles, and no matter how many times I tried, I couldn't get past the sift. It was frustrating because I knew I had the skills and experience — I just didn't know how to communicate them in the right way. Then, I finally cracked the formula.

Once I understood what recruiters were *really* looking for — how to write behaviour statements using the STAR format properly, how to match the Success Profile behaviours to my examples, how to be specific instead of vague — everything changed.

With the exact same skills, experience, and background, I applied again — this time for a Senior Executive Officer (**SEO**) role. And I got it.

That shift wasn't about becoming more qualified — it was about learning how to articulate my experience in the way the system recognises and rewards.

That's why I wrote this guide: to help you do the same.

This isn't a fluffy, theoretical book full of HR buzzwords. It's a straightforward, practical walkthrough for people who want to land a real job at **EO**, **HEO**, or **SEO** level — without the guesswork.

Whether you're:

- Trying to get your first foot in the door
- Switching careers from the private sector
- Or just tired of getting sifted out with no feedback

...this book will help you understand what's going wrong, and what to do differently.

We'll cover the full process:

✅ **Success Profiles and how they really work**

✅ **Writing strong behaviour statements that actually pass the sift**

✅ **Preparing for Civil Service interviews (and handling the weird questions)**

✅ **Common mistakes and how to avoid them**

✅ **Templates and checklists to keep you on track**

No nonsense. No fluff. Just advice that works.

Ready to finally get that "Congratulations" email?

Let's get started.

Chapter 1: The Civil Service Landscape

Before we dive into writing behaviour statements or preparing for interviews, it's helpful to understand the structure of the Civil Service itself — and where **EO**, **HEO**, and **SEO** roles fit in.

Many people apply without fully realising what these grades actually involve, or how they relate to the wider organisation. Knowing this doesn't just make you more informed — it makes your application stronger, too. You'll be able to tailor your examples to the expectations of the role and show that you *understand the job*.

Let's break it down.

What Is the Civil Service?

The UK Civil Service is made up of the people who support the government in delivering public services, developing policies, and keeping the country running behind the scenes. These aren't political roles — civil servants are expected to remain impartial, no matter which party is in power.

If you've ever applied for a passport, claimed benefits, filed your taxes, or needed help from a government department, you've interacted with the work of civil servants — often without realising it.

Civil servants work across **hundreds of departments, agencies, and public bodies**. Some roles are highly specialised (like economists, scientists, or policy analysts), but most fall into generalist roles involving casework, admin, communications, project delivery, or policy support.

The Civil Service is often described as the **"engine room" of government** — quietly keeping things moving in the background. It's one of the largest employers in the UK, with jobs ranging from junior administrative assistants to senior directors working on national strategy.

It's Not Like a Private Company

The Civil Service isn't one single organisation with one CEO — it's a vast network of departments (like HMRC, DWP, and the Home Office) and smaller teams within them. Each area focuses on different services and goals, but they're all part of the same overall system.

Importantly, while the day-to-day work can vary massively from one role to another, the **recruitment process is centralised** through the Civil Service Jobs platform — and most departments follow the same **Success Profiles framework**, which includes behaviours, strengths, and experience-based assessments.

That means once you understand how the system works, you can apply for roles across different departments using a consistent approach — and build your career over time.

Examples of Civil Service Departments and What They Do

The list below highlights some of the biggest departments within the Civil Service, along with a quick explanation of what each one is responsible for. This can help you understand where your skills might fit — and give you a sense of what kinds of work civil servants actually do.

DEPARTMENT	WHAT THEY DO
DEPARTMENT FOR WORK AND PENSIONS (DWP)	Handles benefits like Universal Credit, pensions, and job support
HM REVENUE & CUSTOMS (HMRC)	Manages taxes, VAT, customs, and tax credits
HOME OFFICE	Deals with immigration, visas, policing, and national security
DEPARTMENT OF HEALTH AND SOCIAL CARE (DHSC)	Oversees NHS policy, public health, and social care reform
MINISTRY OF JUSTICE (MOJ)	Manages prisons, courts, probation, and legal aid systems
DEPARTMENT FOR EDUCATION (DFE)	Responsible for schools, early years, and higher education
DEPARTMENT FOR ENERGY SECURITY AND NET ZERO	Works on energy policy, climate change, and net zero targets
CABINET OFFICE	Coordinates across government, civil service reform, and emergency planning
FOREIGN, COMMONWEALTH & DEVELOPMENT OFFICE (FCDO)	Manages diplomacy, foreign aid, and international development
DEPARTMENT FOR BUSINESS AND TRADE (DBT)	Supports business growth, trade deals, and economic policy

These are just a few of the biggest departments — there are also **agencies, regulators, and public bodies** working on everything from food safety to driving tests.

You can explore more departments and job types by visiting:
https://www.civilservicejobs.service.gov.uk/csr/index.cgi

Understanding the Grading Structure

The Civil Service uses a grading system alongside job titles, which can sometimes be a bit confusing if you're new to it. Instead of just seeing titles like "Project Manager" or "HR Officer," you'll also see grades such as **EO, HEO,** or **SEO** listed with the role. These grades help indicate the level of responsibility, seniority, and corresponding pay scale within the organisation.

#Here's a quick overview of the **most common grades**:

GRADE	EQUIVALENT LEVEL
AA / AO	Entry-level
EO	Junior management
HEO	Middle management
SEO	Senior operational
G7 / G6	Strategic leadership

The focus of this book is **EO, HEO,** and **SEO** — the "meaty middle" of the Civil Service, where most external recruitment takes place.

What to Expect at Each Level

The Civil Service is made up of many grades — but for most external applicants, the most common roles you'll come across are **Executive Officer (EO), Higher Executive Officer (HEO),** and **Senior Executive Officer (SEO).**

Understanding what each level typically involves doesn't just help you choose the right jobs — it helps you tailor your application, examples, and interview answers to **match the expectations of the grade**.

Below is a practical summary of what recruiters are looking for at each level — including the kind of work involved and what matters at application stage.

Executive Officer (EO)

EO roles are often the first point of entry for people joining from outside the Civil Service. These roles involve delivering core services, supporting frontline work, and managing individual tasks or cases with care and consistency.

Typical responsibilities:
- Delivering day-to-day casework, administrative tasks, or service operations
- Responding to public enquiries or processing applications

- Following procedures accurately and escalating when needed
- Supporting or occasionally supervising junior team members

✅ At this level, **attention to detail, communication skills, and reliability** are key.

What matters at application stage:

- Showing you can handle responsibility and follow procedures
- Communicating clearly, both in writing and in person
- Demonstrating teamwork, reliability, and good judgement
- Giving examples that show independence (without needing constant supervision)

🎯 Think: Have you managed a process, delivered work accurately, or helped improve a system?

● Higher Executive Officer (HEO)

HEO roles are a step up from EO, often involving more ownership, problem-solving, and interaction with a wider range of people. You might lead on small projects, oversee a workstream, or act as the go-to person in your team for a particular topic.

Typical responsibilities:

- Managing complex cases or delivering operational improvements
- Writing briefings or reports that support decision-making
- Leading a small team or mentoring more junior staff
- Collaborating with external stakeholders or internal partners
- Reviewing data, identifying risks, and making informed recommendations

✅ At this level, **autonomy, initiative, and strategic thinking** become more important.

What matters at application stage:

- Showing you can work independently and manage competing priorities
- Using evidence to support your decisions
- Demonstrating leadership behaviours — even informally
- Writing clearly, concisely, and persuasively

🎯 Think: Have you improved a process, solved a tricky issue, or led a piece of work to completion?

Senior Executive Officer (SEO)

SEO roles involve more responsibility and oversight. You'll often be the key decision-maker for a programme, team, or policy area — with a mix of delivery, strategy, and leadership.

Typical responsibilities:

- Overseeing multiple projects, deadlines, or workstreams
- Leading teams through change or uncertainty
- Managing stakeholder relationships at a senior level
- Making decisions that carry reputational, financial, or operational risk
- Acting as a strategic adviser within your area

At this level, **strong leadership, judgement, and communication** are essential.

What matters at application stage:

- Demonstrating confidence in decision-making and leading others
- Showing that you can prioritise effectively and balance competing pressures
- Communicating clearly and persuasively with senior audiences
- Highlighting your ability to manage complexity and deliver through others

Think: Have you led a team, shaped a strategy, or handled a high-risk or high-impact project?

Why This Matters for You

When applying, it's easy to treat **EO**, **HEO**, and **SEO** roles as just "Civil Service jobs." But the expectations shift quite a bit between grades — and tailoring your application to the right level is one of the biggest things that can make or break your success.

If you're applying for an **SEO** role and writing behaviour statements that sound like an **EO**, you'll likely fall short — even if your experience is excellent.

I remember when I was applying for my current role in the Department for Education. The job advert was really cryptic. It gave a vague overview of responsibilities, mentioned a few behaviours, and didn't give much away about the day-to-day work. I found it hard to prepare — not because I wasn't capable, but because I wasn't entirely sure what they wanted.

And that's the thing: a lot of Civil Service job adverts are intentionally broad or unclear. In many cases, that's due to confidentiality (especially when the role involves sensitive government work), or simply because teams want to keep flexibility in how they fill posts. But it can be incredibly frustrating as an applicant.

That's why it's even more important to understand what each grade typically involves — because the advert won't always spell it out. The clearer *you* are on what's expected, the more targeted and effective your behaviour examples will be.

Later in this book, we'll walk through how to adjust your examples based on the level you're applying for, and how to show the right blend of autonomy, leadership, and impact — even when the job description gives you next to nothing.

Real Examples of Civil Service Jobs at Each Grade

To help you get a clearer picture of what roles look like in real life, here are some example job titles you might see advertised — along with short descriptions of what those roles typically involve.

These are just examples. Every department may name things slightly differently, but the core responsibilities tend to be similar across government.

Executive Officer (EO)

JOB TITLE	WHAT IT TYPICALLY INVOLVES
UNIVERSAL CREDIT CASEWORKER	Assessing claims, supporting customers, and making benefit decisions
PASSPORT OPERATIONS OFFICER	Checking documents and processing passport applications
ADMINISTRATIVE OFFICER (COURTS)	Supporting court hearings and managing legal paperwork
CONTACT CENTRE ADVISOR	Answering calls, updating records, and giving clear public advice

Higher Executive Officer (HEO)

JOB TITLE	WHAT IT TYPICALLY INVOLVES
POLICY OFFICER	Writing briefings, analysing issues, and supporting policy development
BUSINESS CHANGE OFFICER	Leading small projects to improve how a service or team works
PROGRAMME SUPPORT OFFICER	Coordinating activity across a programme and reporting on progress
STAKEHOLDER ENGAGEMENT MANAGER	Liaising with partners, charities, or public bodies on key issues

🔵 Senior Executive Officer (SEO)

JOB TITLE	WHAT IT TYPICALLY INVOLVES
DELIVERY MANAGER	Leading a team to implement a service or digital product
SENIOR POLICY ADVISER	Shaping strategy, managing risks, and briefing ministers
OPERATIONAL TEAM LEADER	Overseeing multiple casework teams and reporting on delivery
PROGRAMME LEAD (STRATEGY & REFORM)	Coordinating national-level changes and engaging senior stakeholders

✅ In Summary

- EO, HEO, and SEO roles sit in the middle of the Civil Service structure — where a lot of important delivery and coordination happens.

- Each grade comes with different expectations — the higher the grade, the more strategic and leadership-focused the role becomes.

- Understanding these expectations helps you tailor your application and give recruiters what they're looking for.

Chapter 2: Demystifying Success Profiles

One of the first things you'll see in any Civil Service job advert — right after the vague job title — is a reference to something called **Success Profiles**. For most people, this is where the confusion really starts.

You might be thinking: *What are these? How do I use them? Do I need to meet all five parts?*

Let's clear it up right now.

What Are Success Profiles?

When you apply for a Civil Service job, you'll be assessed using something called the **Success Profiles framework**.

This might sound like internal jargon — but don't worry. Once you understand what it means, it becomes a lot easier to write your application and prepare for interviews.

The key idea behind Success Profiles is this:

Instead of focusing just on your qualifications or job titles, the Civil Service looks at the qualities that make someone good at the job.

It's designed to give people from all backgrounds a fair shot — even if they've never worked in government before.

Rather than saying, "You must have X years of experience doing Y," recruiters want to see **how you think, how you work, and how you behave in real situations**.

The Five Elements of Success Profiles

There are five elements that may be used in an application:

1. **Behaviours** – How you've acted in specific situations
2. **Strengths** – How you naturally work and respond to challenges
3. **Experience** – What you've done before and what skills you bring
4. **Ability** – How well you perform in a particular task or test
5. **Technical** – Specialist knowledge required for certain roles

✦ **But here's the part most people miss:**
☞ **Not all five elements are used in every application.**

Each job will list which elements apply — usually in the job advert or the candidate pack. Some roles focus heavily on **behaviours and strengths**, while others may include **technical skills or online tests**.

That's why it's important to always read the job advert carefully and make sure you know what they're assessing. Once you understand the Success Profiles in play, you can tailor your answers to match them — and avoid wasting time on things that won't be scored.

✦ **The Most Common Success Profile Elements (for EO–SEO)**

For most roles at **Executive Officer (EO)**, **Higher Executive Officer (HEO)**, and **Senior Executive Officer (SEO)** level, your application will focus on **three main Success Profile elements**:

☑ **Behaviours**

These are often the most important part of your application — and the part people find hardest. They're designed to assess **how you've acted in past situations**, using real examples from your work, volunteering, or life experience.

Each behaviour has an official description (like "Communicating and Influencing" or "Working Together") that outlines what good performance looks like.

You'll usually be asked to:

- Write short behaviour statements (often 250 words each)
- Use a specific structure (e.g. STAR — Situation, Task, Action, Result)
- Focus on outcomes and your personal contribution

✦ **Tip:** Even if a job doesn't ask for a formal personal statement, your behaviour examples are still the main part of your written application — and they're scored closely against the Civil Service behaviours framework.

☑ **Strengths**

Strengths are about **how you naturally think, feel, and work**. Rather than judging whether you're "right" or "wrong," strength-based questions explore what motivates you and how you're likely to behave day-to-day.

They're often assessed at interview and delivered in a **quick-fire format** — for example:

- "Are you someone who likes routine or variety?"
- "Do you prefer working alone or as part of a team?"
- "What energises you at work?"

There's no trick — but the aim is to find people who are a good **natural fit for the role**. For example, a job that involves constant change might favour someone who enjoys variety, while a policy role may look for people who like detail and analysis.

Tip: Be honest. If you try to "guess" what they want, you'll sound scripted. Strengths answers work best when they're authentic.

Experience

Experience still matters — just not in the way you might expect.

You don't need to have worked in government (or even in the same industry) to get a Civil Service job. What matters is that you can show **transferable experience**: skills or achievements that relate to the role.

You might be assessed on experience in two main ways:

- Through a **personal statement**, where you explain your relevant background
- Through your **behaviour examples**, which naturally draw on past roles

Example:

If a role asks for someone with "strong stakeholder engagement skills," you could draw on experience from a customer service job, a volunteer role, or managing relationships in a past project.

Tip: Civil Service recruiters care less about job titles and more about the impact you made. If you can show that you've taken ownership, solved problems, or worked with others to achieve results — that's experience that counts.

Less Common Success Profile Elements (at EO–SEO)

While most EO, HEO, and SEO applications focus on **Behaviours, Strengths, and Experience**, there are two other Success Profile elements that may appear occasionally — but are **less common** at these levels:

✗ Ability

This refers to **aptitude or skills tests** — things like:

- Verbal reasoning

- Numerical reasoning
- Situational judgement
- Work-based exercises or timed tests

You're more likely to come across these in:

- Entry-level roles (especially AA or AO)
- Large-volume recruitment campaigns
- Certain fast-track or graduate schemes

At EO–SEO level, ability testing is often **used as a sift stage** — meaning it's used to reduce the number of applicants before assessing written answers. If this applies, it'll usually be **clearly stated in the job advert**, and you'll be sent a link to complete the test online.

Tip: If you're asked to complete one of these tests, there are practice versions available online — and you should treat it seriously. These tests are timed and scored automatically, so preparation matters.

✘ Technical

Technical is only used for roles that require **specialist knowledge or qualifications** — such as:

- Finance (e.g. accountant, audit, procurement)
- Digital and IT (e.g. software engineer, cyber security analyst)
- Engineering, legal, or scientific roles

These jobs will often state that you need to demonstrate **technical skills or credentials**, such as a specific qualification or membership of a professional body.

If technical skills are part of the Success Profile, the job description will:

- State it clearly
- List the required qualifications or competencies
- Sometimes ask for evidence at application stage or interview

Most generalist EO, HEO, and SEO roles won't include this — but if they do, it won't be hidden. You'll know upfront.

📌 Final Thought:

If a role doesn't mention **Ability** or **Technical**, you don't need to address them — and they won't form part of your score.

Focus your energy on what **is** being assessed. That's where you can make an impact.

Where You'll See Success Profiles in Action

Success Profiles shape the entire Civil Service recruitment process — from the moment you see a job advert to the day you sit your interview. But if you don't know what to look for, it's easy to miss how they're being used.

Here's where and how you'll typically encounter them:

In the Job Advert or Candidate Pack

Most job listings on Civil Service Jobs include a section titled "Success Profiles" or "Assessment Methods."

This is where you'll find:

- The **behaviours** being assessed (e.g. "Communicating and Influencing")
- Whether **strengths or experience** will be part of the assessment
- Any tests or technical requirements

It may be written in brief bullet points, or laid out in a table. Some adverts also include a link to a **candidate information pack**, which goes into more detail.

📌 **Tip:** Don't skim this section — it tells you exactly what to focus on in your application.

On the Application Form

When you apply online, you'll usually be asked to provide:

- **Behaviour statements** (often 250 words per behaviour)
- **A personal statement** or **supporting information** (sometimes optional)
- Occasionally, **evidence of experience** or a CV

Each written section will be assessed according to the Success Profiles listed in the advert — and scored by trained reviewers using a marking framework.

📎 **Tip:** Everything you write should be tailored to those profiles. If "Working Together" is one of the behaviours listed, don't just mention teamwork in passing — give a specific example that shows it clearly.

🎙 At Interview

Civil Service interviews almost always use **structured questions** based on Success Profiles. You'll usually be told in advance which behaviours will be covered — and you may be assessed on strengths too.

Expect:

- **Behaviour questions** that start with "Tell me about a time when…"
- **Strength questions** that explore how you like to work
- Sometimes, **follow-up questions** to test your judgement or reasoning

📎 **Tip:** Success Profiles aren't just theory — they shape every part of the process. Once you learn how to "read between the lines," you'll start to see exactly what the assessors are looking for.

💭 Pro Tip:

Even if the job advert feels vague, once you understand Success Profiles, you can **reverse-engineer the expectations**. That means writing stronger examples, giving better interviews, and standing out from applicants who are still guessing.

💭 A Closer Look at Behaviours

If there's one part of the application that trips people up the most, it's behaviours.

That's because the Civil Service uses specific behaviour "definitions" — often written in broad, idealistic terms — and expects you to provide **real examples** that prove you've demonstrated those behaviours in action.

Each behaviour outlines **how a successful civil servant should act** in a particular area. These apply across departments and job types, which means they're designed to be flexible — but that also makes them feel vague if you're new to the system.

🎯 Example Behaviour: *Communicating and Influencing*

Let's take one of the most common behaviours as an example. The official wording might look like this:

"Communicate purpose and direction with clarity, integrity and enthusiasm. Respect the needs, responses and opinions of others."

That sounds great — but... what does that mean in real life?

It could apply to:

- Giving clear updates to a colleague
- Handling a complaint calmly
- Writing a briefing that helps others make decisions
- Persuading someone to support your idea
- Adjusting how you communicate based on who you're speaking to

The behaviour definition gives you the **theme**, but not the detail. It's your job to **turn that theme into a real situation** — and to show what *you* did, how you did it, and what the result was.

🧱 How to Make It Work for You

You'll learn how to structure your examples in the next chapter using the **STAR format** — but for now, just keep this in mind:

☑ Your example should focus on **one situation**
☑ It should show **your personal contribution** — not just what the team did
☑ It should lead to a **clear outcome** or result
☑ You don't need to demonstrate **every word** of the behaviour definition — just enough to show you meet the standard

---

🗣 Real talk:

Most people who fail Civil Service applications don't fail because they're not good enough. They fail because they wrote something too general, too vague, or too far below the level of the role.

That's why understanding how to handle behaviours is so important — and why the next chapter is all about helping you write them well.

What Changes Between Grades?

Here's where a lot of applicants go wrong — not because they're bad at their jobs, but because they don't realise that **the same behaviour is assessed differently at each grade.**

The Civil Service uses **the same core behaviours** across many roles. You'll often see things like:

- Communicating and Influencing
- Working Together
- Making Effective Decisions
- Managing a Quality Service

These appear whether you're applying for EO, HEO, or SEO. But here's the crucial bit:

The behaviours stay the same — but the expectations get higher.

Same Behaviour, Different Level

Let's take a basic example — "Working Together."

- At **EO level**, you might show how you cooperated with a colleague to meet a deadline or resolved a misunderstanding in your team.
- At **HEO level**, you'd be expected to show how you brought together different viewpoints, maybe across departments, to achieve a shared goal.
- At **SEO level**, you should be demonstrating leadership — like how you influenced senior stakeholders or aligned multiple teams to deliver a strategic outcome.

It's not about choosing a *better* example — it's about showing a **wider impact, greater responsibility, and more complex decision-making** as the grades increase.

Common Pitfall: Writing Below the Level

One of the most common reasons good candidates don't get shortlisted is this:

They give solid examples — but those examples sound **too junior** for the job they've applied for.

For instance:

- A HEO applicant talks about "helping their manager solve a problem" instead of owning a solution themselves

- An SEO applicant writes about "working as part of a team" instead of **leading, prioritising,** or **guiding others**

This isn't just about confidence — it's about **choosing examples that match the grade's expectations.**

📌 **Tip:** Ask yourself:

"If someone at this level was doing this job well, what would I expect them to do?"

Then choose an example that matches that level of thinking, responsibility, and outcome.

✅ **In Summary**

- **Success Profiles are the Civil Service's way of assessing candidates — they focus on Behaviours, Strengths, and Experience (primarily at EO–SEO).**
- **Job ads will tell you which elements apply — though not always clearly.**
- **Behaviours are the most important part of your application, and your examples need to match the level you're applying for.**
- **The STAR format will help you structure your answers — and we'll cover that next.**

Chapter 3: Writing Your Civil Service CV (Experience Section)

⚠ Important: Civil Service Applications Are Anonymous

Before you begin writing, remember that Civil Service applications must be anonymised. You should **not** include any personally identifiable information, such as:

- Your name or job title
- Your educational institution (e.g. "University of Manchester")
- Your age, gender, email address, phone number, or home address
- Your nationality or immigration status

✅ Refer to employers and organisations **generically** (e.g. "a large UK supermarket" or "a local housing charity")

✅ Keep the focus on your **experience, responsibilities, and skill**s — not personal details.

Applications containing personal information may be rejected automatically before they even reach the sift panel.

🎯 What Are They Actually Looking For in the CV Section?

If a Civil Service job advert asks for a CV or "experience" section, it's easy to think of it as just a formality. But in reality, this section plays a key role in helping the panel understand who you are, where you've come from, and how you might fit into the role.

Unlike behaviour examples, this part of the application **isn't always scored in detail**. But it **sets the tone** for how your whole application is received. It gives the panel context, helps them understand your examples more clearly, and lets them see whether you have the kind of background that fits the level and demands of the role.

✅ The Panel Wants to Know:

- What kind of experience you're bringing to the table
- Whether you've done work of similar complexity, pace, or pressure
- Whether your background aligns with the duties and values of the role
- If you have the potential to grow into the role if you're not a perfect match yet

✅ Recommended Paragraph Structure (Bolstered)

Here's a structure that matches what panels expect — and helps you come across as focused, relevant, and ready.

✅ Paragraph 1 – Overview (Who You Are Professionally)

Set the scene with a short, neutral summary of your current or most recent role, including your sector and general level of responsibility.

Include:

- Your current or most recent position (e.g. "I currently work in a customer-facing role within the financial services sector")
- A sentence describing the kind of organisation or service
- An indication of the level you've worked at (e.g. working independently, supervising others, leading tasks, managing projects)

💬 **Tip:** Avoid naming specific employers — especially if they're niche. The panel cares more about *what you do* than *who you do it for*.

Example:
I currently work as a case administrator in a national organisation supporting clients through complex financial situations. I regularly manage my own caseload, prioritise competing demands, and liaise with internal departments to resolve queries efficiently.

✅ Paragraph 2 – Relevant Experience (Tailor to the Job Advert)

This is the most important paragraph. Show the panel that you've read the job advert properly — and that you've got experience that matches the key duties or person specification.

Focus on:

- The tasks you've done that are **similar to those in the advert**
- Any systems, tools, processes, or environments that overlap
- Responsibilities that show you're already operating at (or near) the grade you're applying for

💬 **Tip:** Use language that mirrors the advert. If they say "manage correspondence," say "manage correspondence" — not "respond to emails."

Example:
In my current role, I'm responsible for monitoring and responding to incoming queries, updating case notes, and maintaining accurate records across multiple systems. I often

deal with sensitive information and work to tight deadlines, which has helped me build strong organisational skills and attention to detail.

✅ Paragraph 3 – Strengths and Qualities (Your Working Style)

This is your chance to add a bit more personality — to show how you work, not just what you've done.

Focus on:

- Your natural strengths and working habits
- How you manage pressure, adapt to change, or support others
- Any recognised qualities (e.g. "I've been trusted to…" or "colleagues often turn to me for…")

💬 **Tip:** This shouldn't feel like a list of buzzwords. Give one or two short, credible examples that back up what you're saying.

Example:
I'm someone who thrives in a structured but fast-paced environment. I stay calm under pressure and enjoy finding practical ways to solve problems. I've often been trusted to train new starters or help with service improvements — roles that rely on clear communication and patience.

✅ Paragraph 4 – Fit for the Role and the Civil Service

Close with a short paragraph that explains **why you're applying** — and why this job makes sense for you.

Include:

- How your experience and values align with the role
- What attracts you to the Civil Service (or public service more broadly)
- A quick nod to the department's purpose, values, or work — to show you've done your research

💬 **Tip:** This isn't your full personal statement — just a confident, positive wrap-up.

Example:
I'm drawn to this role because it builds on my experience while giving me the chance to contribute to public service. I value clear processes, fairness, and the opportunity to support people through difficult circumstances — all of which align with the department's mission.

Civil Service CV Example: EO Caseworker

Example Job Advert Summary

Role Title: Executive Officer (**EO**) – Caseworker
Department: Home Office
Location: Various UK locations
Salary: £27,000–£29,000
Working pattern: Full-time, flexible working available

Job Description (Summarised from a Realistic Advert)

You will work as part of an operational delivery team, processing and managing cases relating to visa applications and immigration decisions. You will need to work accurately, follow clear processes, and communicate decisions clearly and compassionately to members of the public.

Responsibilities

- Review and manage case files to ensure accurate and timely decisions
- Liaise with other departments and stakeholders to gather information
- Communicate with applicants by letter, email, or phone
- Maintain accurate records using internal systems
- Follow policy guidance and operational processes
- Escalate complex or sensitive cases where appropriate

Essential Criteria

- Experience working in a fast-paced administrative or customer-focused role
- Ability to manage competing tasks and priorities
- Strong written and verbal communication skills
- Attention to detail and a commitment to accuracy
- Good IT skills and ability to use databases or case management systems
- Professionalism and sensitivity when handling personal information

✨ Example CV – EO Caseworker (Approx. 350 Words)

I currently work as a Support Officer at a community advice charity, where I manage client enquiries, support vulnerable service users, and maintain accurate records of case interactions. I've held this role for two years, and previously worked in administrative and customer service roles within a local authority and the care sector.

In my current position, I manage a caseload of up to 30 clients per week, often dealing with complex or sensitive issues including housing, benefits, and legal support. I communicate with clients by phone, email, and in person, explaining processes clearly and helping them gather evidence for their cases. I am responsible for updating our case management system daily, producing support letters, and maintaining strict confidentiality. I also work closely with external agencies to coordinate referrals or gather supporting information, and escalate safeguarding concerns where needed.

I'm confident working under pressure, managing changing priorities, and following organisational processes to ensure tasks are completed accurately and on time. I have strong written communication skills, and I'm regularly asked to help draft letters and review case files for colleagues. I enjoy problem-solving and I'm highly motivated to help people navigate complex systems.

I'm now looking to take on a new challenge in the Civil Service, and believe my experience aligns well with the responsibilities of the **EO** Caseworker role. I have relevant case handling experience, am confident using internal systems, and am comfortable working in environments that require professionalism, empathy, and discretion.

✅ **This CV directly reflects:**

- The **essential criteria** (case handling, communication, accuracy, discretion)
- The **day-to-day responsibilities** (record-keeping, client contact, liaison with other teams)
- **Transferable skills** from outside the Civil Service, tailored into public-sector language

---

Civil Service CV Example: HEO Business Support Officer

Example Job Advert Summary

Role Title: Higher Executive Officer (**HEO**) – Business Support Officer
Department: Department for Business and Trade
Location: Hybrid – London or regional offices
Salary: £32,000–£36,000

Job Description (Summarised)

You will play a key role in supporting operational delivery across the department. This includes coordinating internal governance, supporting senior leadership teams, overseeing planning and reporting cycles, and managing business-critical processes. You'll work across teams and functions, requiring excellent organisation, stakeholder management, and problem-solving skills.

Key Responsibilities

- Manage business planning and reporting processes
- Prepare briefings, trackers, and status updates for senior managers
- Maintain oversight of team activities and priorities
- Liaise with internal and external stakeholders to support delivery
- Identify process improvements and support change implementation
- Monitor risks, escalations, and team-level governance

Essential Criteria

- Experience coordinating operational or business support functions
- Strong written communication skills (e.g. producing summaries or reports)
- Excellent organisational skills, able to manage multiple priorities
- Confidence engaging with senior stakeholders
- Proactive, solutions-focused working style
- Ability to work flexibly across teams

HEO CV Example – Business Support Officer (Approx. 400 Words)

I currently work as a Regional Support Coordinator for a UK-wide skills charity. I've held this role for just over two years, and prior to that I worked in local government and adult education delivery. My experience has primarily focused on operations, stakeholder coordination, and project tracking — all within fast-paced, multi-partner environments.

In my current role, I act as the central coordination point for three regional teams delivering training programmes to jobseekers and low-income learners. I oversee delivery schedules, collate performance and finance data from each delivery partner, and compile monthly reports for our programme leads. I regularly produce briefings, prepare meeting packs, and draft updates for senior funders. I also manage the regional inbox and act as the first point of contact for external queries.

I work closely with delivery leads to monitor risks, escalate delays, and help teams stay on track with funding conditions. I've introduced a shared reporting tracker which reduced duplication and improved data quality. I'm confident coordinating across teams, building strong working relationships, and adapting quickly when plans or funding cycles shift.

I'm highly organised and comfortable managing multiple priorities at once. I have strong written communication skills and am often asked to proof or quality check reports before submission. I work well under pressure, am confident using Excel and Microsoft 365 tools, and enjoy supporting senior leaders with reliable, responsive input.

I'm now looking to bring my coordination, reporting, and stakeholder engagement skills into the Civil Service. The **HEO** Business Support Officer role aligns closely with my experience — particularly in relation to supporting governance, improving internal systems, and ensuring operational work runs smoothly.

This CV shows clear alignment with:

- The **essential criteria** (coordination, communication, stakeholder engagement)
- The **day-to-day responsibilities** (planning, reporting, inboxes, risk tracking)
- A **confident, professional tone** without relying on Civil Service experience

Civil Service CV Example: SEO Project Manager

Example Job Advert Summary

Role Title: Senior Executive Officer (**SEO**) – Project Manager
Department: Department for Levelling Up, Housing and Communities
Location: Flexible, with some travel to regional sites
Salary: £41,000–£45,000

Job Description (Summarised)

You will manage and oversee delivery of funded infrastructure or regeneration projects. You'll be responsible for monitoring delivery risks, managing key relationships, and ensuring programme objectives are achieved. This role involves working across government teams, external delivery partners, and local authorities to keep high-profile projects on track.

Key Responsibilities

- Manage day-to-day oversight of a portfolio of infrastructure or capital projects
- Work with delivery partners to ensure milestones are met and risks are addressed
- Represent the department in stakeholder meetings
- Draft briefings, reporting updates, and delivery recommendations
- Monitor budgets, timelines, and key performance indicators
- Contribute to governance reporting and programme reviews

Essential Criteria

- Experience managing delivery of complex or multi-stakeholder projects
- Strong organisational and planning skills
- Ability to monitor risk, performance, and outcomes
- Excellent written and verbal communication
- Confidence engaging with senior stakeholders
- Ability to represent an organisation professionally and diplomatically

SEO CV Example – Project Manager (Approx. 400 Words)

I currently work as a **Programme Delivery Manager** for a housing and regeneration consultancy that supports local government clients to deliver public-sector funded infrastructure programmes. I've worked in this role for three years, following a background in programme support and operational project management across the voluntary and built environment sectors.

In my current role, I manage a portfolio of capital-funded regeneration projects across five local authorities. I work closely with council teams, housing providers, and external contractors to monitor progress, flag delivery risks, and provide assurance to funders. I coordinate monthly progress reviews, track budgets and milestones, and produce delivery summaries and risk logs for client briefings. I've led workshops to help delivery partners improve reporting quality and proactively identified early delivery risks which were escalated and resolved before they impacted funding timelines.

I am confident engaging with senior stakeholders, both in writing and in person. I often represent our organisation at client meetings, prepare short strategic updates, and lead discussions around delivery risks and contingency planning. I work flexibly across programmes and adapt my approach depending on the partner and context. I have also worked closely with internal teams to streamline our project documentation and introduced a shared tracker to improve visibility across workstreams.

I am highly organised, solutions-focused, and experienced working in complex, multi-stakeholder environments. I enjoy supporting projects that have a clear public value and am used to navigating the balance between delivery, compliance, and long-term outcomes.

I am now looking to bring this experience into the Civil Service, where I believe I can contribute to successful project delivery and help support teams working across complex funding, infrastructure, or place-based programmes. The **SEO** Project Manager role aligns closely with my current experience, and I'm enthusiastic about the opportunity to work in a public sector leadership role.

This CV demonstrates:
- Leadership and **oversight of delivery**
- Experience with **reporting, risk, and stakeholder engagement**
- A clear match to the **essential criteria and responsibilities**
- Strong potential for **stepping into the Civil Service** from a relevant background

Chapter 4: Writing a Strong Personal Statement

Some Civil Service roles will ask you to submit a **Personal Statement** as part of your application. This is separate from your CV and behaviour examples — and it's often the most misunderstood section.

Applicants frequently ask:

- *"Is this the same as a cover letter?"*
- *"Should I repeat my behaviours?"*
- *"Is it meant to be personal, like a life story?"*

Let's clear that up right now.

🎯 What Is the Personal Statement For?

The **Personal Statement** is one of the most important — and often misunderstood — parts of a Civil Service application.

While your behaviour examples follow a specific format and focus on individual skills or actions, the personal statement is your opportunity to **step back and connect the dots**. It's where you explain why you're a strong, well-rounded match for the role as a whole.

You're not tied to STAR structure here. Instead, think of this section as your **narrative** — your chance to walk the panel through:

- What you bring to the table
- Why you're applying
- And how your background makes sense for this particular job

---

📌 It's your opportunity to:

- ☑ **Demonstrate your understanding of the role**
  Show that you've read the job description and understand what the team needs. This doesn't mean repeating the advert — it means reflecting it in your language, tone, and examples.

- ☑ **Show how your experience aligns with the responsibilities and essential criteria**
  You don't need to list everything you've ever done — but highlight the parts of your experience that directly match the duties or skills mentioned.

- ✅ **Highlight your motivation for applying and joining the Civil Service**
  This is your chance to go beyond the technical fit and show your values, purpose, and interest in public service — even if it's your first time applying.

🔖 **Why it matters:** Even if the personal statement isn't scored separately, it shapes how assessors view your behaviour examples and overall application. It gives them context and confidence that you understand what the job involves — and that you're someone worth progressing to the next stage.

📋 **What's the Word Count – and How Much Should You Write?**

The word count for a personal statement usually depends on the **grade and department**, but typical ranges are:

GRADE	TYPICAL WORD COUNT
EO	500–750 words
HEO	750–1,000 words
SEO	1,000–1,250 words

The application form will clearly state the maximum word count — and you won't be able to submit more than that.

❓ **Should You Write as Much as Possible?**

Not necessarily.
It's a common myth that you should always write right up to the word limit — but in reality, **quality matters far more than quantity.**

✅ **Aim for:**

- Clear, well-structured paragraphs
- Evidence that links to the role
- A confident, readable tone

🚫 Don't pad your statement with filler just to reach the word limit. A sharp, tailored 800-word statement will outperform a 1,249-word waffle every time.

🔍 **Tip: A good range is 85–95% of the word limit. That shows you've made the most of the space without rambling.**

⚠ Anonymity Reminder

As with all parts of your application, the personal statement must be fully anonymised.

✗ Do not include:

- Your name, age, address, contact details
- Specific job titles (e.g. "Shift Leader at Tesco")
- School/university names
- Nationality or immigration status

☑ Use general descriptions instead, e.g.:

"I currently work as a manager in a national retail organisation…"

☑ Structure That Works

There's no perfect formula for a personal statement — but if you're not sure where to start, this **four-part structure** is simple, effective, and aligns with what Civil Service panels are looking for.

It helps you stay focused, avoid rambling, and make a clear case for why you're a great fit for the job.

---

1. Introduction – Who you are professionally and what attracted you to the role

Start strong with a short paragraph that sets the scene. Mention:

- Your current or most recent role
- Your general background or career journey (e.g. customer service, admin, retail, care)
- A sentence on what drew you to this opportunity

💬 **Tip:** Keep it factual and warm — not too casual, but not robotic either.

Example: I currently work in a busy administrative role within a national organisation. I've developed a strong foundation in managing data, dealing with public enquiries, and supporting service delivery. I'm now looking to apply my skills in a role that offers greater purpose and public impact, which is what attracted me to this opportunity.

2. Relevant Experience – Link your previous roles to the job's key duties or criteria

This is the core of your statement. Pull out the experience that **most closely matches** the role you're applying for.

Focus on:

- Similar tasks or responsibilities
- Relevant systems, tools, or processes
- Transferable experience from other sectors or contexts

📌 **Tip:** Use the job advert as your guide. If they mention "managing competing priorities" or "working with sensitive information," make sure you mention when you've done that — ideally using their language.

In my current role, I handle a high volume of casework, manage competing priorities, and update internal systems with accuracy. I've become confident working under pressure while keeping a strong focus on detail and customer care.

---

3. Skills & Strengths – Highlight your working style and transferable qualities

Use this paragraph to give the panel a sense of **how you work** — not just what you've done.

This might include:

- Your communication or teamwork style
- How you manage time, pressure, or change
- Traits others rely on you for (e.g. calmness, problem-solving, organisation)

💭 **Tip:** Think about what colleagues or managers would say about you — and back it up with a quick example where possible.

I'm someone who enjoys improving systems and supporting others. I've often been trusted to train new colleagues or help smooth out inefficient processes. I work best in fast-paced environments and take pride in staying calm and clear under pressure.

---

4. Motivation – Show why you want this role and how you'd contribute

Finish with a short paragraph that makes your interest clear — and connects your values to the role or department.

Include:

- Why this role appeals to you

- Why the Civil Service or public service feels like a good fit
- A brief nod to the department's wider purpose, if appropriate

Tip: You don't need to sound like you've always dreamed of this job — just show that you've thought about it and that you're intentional about applying.

I'm motivated by work that has real purpose and impact. I believe my experience, reliability, and commitment to fairness align well with the values of the Civil Service, and I'm excited by the opportunity to contribute to the work of [Department Name].

Example 1: EO – Caseworker (Approx. 750 words)

I currently work as a Support Officer in a national community advice charity, where I manage client cases, coordinate information, and support vulnerable individuals with a wide range of needs. My background includes customer service and local authority work, all of which have developed my ability to handle sensitive information, remain calm under pressure, and communicate clearly with people from different backgrounds. I'm now looking to bring these skills into the Civil Service, particularly in a role focused on structured casework, fair decision-making, and public service delivery.

In my current role, I handle a high volume of client interactions each week. This involves logging enquiries accurately, reviewing evidence, and helping individuals complete forms or appeals. I maintain clear records on our case management system, follow strict data protection rules, and regularly update third-party organisations where clients have given consent. This experience aligns closely with the responsibilities of an **EO** Caseworker, especially in relation to handling case files, following policy processes, and communicating with members of the public in a sensitive and professional manner.

I am confident following structured guidance, and I'm quick to learn new systems and processes. I recently supported the implementation of a new referral platform, providing feedback to improve its usability and helping team members adjust to the new workflow. I also act as a point of contact for external stakeholders such as housing officers or support workers, helping them access accurate information on client cases and providing updates when authorised to do so.

Written communication is a key part of my role. I regularly draft client letters and internal notes to explain decisions or record key actions. I understand the importance of using clear, neutral language — especially when dealing with sensitive or emotionally charged situations. I have also received positive feedback from clients and colleagues for my calm and professional manner in difficult conversations.

I'm used to working under pressure, and I'm comfortable managing multiple cases at once while meeting internal deadlines and maintaining high standards. I've developed effective time management skills and use checklists and reminders to ensure nothing is missed. I also work closely with my line manager to raise concerns or flag cases that need escalation.

I'm drawn to this Civil Service role because I want to contribute to public service in a meaningful way, particularly in a position where fairness, consistency, and integrity are central to the role. I believe my experience has prepared me well to work within a structured process, handle confidential information with care, and make decisions that affect people's lives. I'm motivated, adaptable, and eager to take on a new challenge in an organisation with a strong reputation for development and progression.

✦ Example 2: HEO – Business Support Officer (Approx. 850 words)

I currently work as a Regional Support Coordinator for a UK-wide skills charity, where I oversee programme delivery across multiple regions. My background spans project coordination, local government, and adult education — all in roles that have required careful stakeholder management, data monitoring, and high-quality reporting. I'm now keen to transition into the Civil Service, where I can apply my experience in an operational support role with national impact.

In my current role, I act as the coordination point between delivery partners, regional managers, and central office colleagues. I'm responsible for producing monthly delivery reports, tracking performance data, preparing briefings, and escalating delivery risks. I introduced a shared tracking system that improved data consistency across three delivery regions and streamlined our monthly reporting cycle. I've also supported strategic reviews by compiling summaries and insights that helped senior colleagues make planning decisions.

I manage the regional inbox, log incoming queries, and respond to day-to-day requests from external stakeholders. I've built a reputation for being reliable, responsive, and solutions-focused. This aligns well with the Business Support Officer role's emphasis on coordination, communication, and enabling others to deliver effectively.

I regularly prepare short written briefings, meeting packs, and slide decks — often at short notice. I'm confident tailoring information for different audiences and am experienced in using Excel, Word, PowerPoint, and collaborative planning tools like Teams and SharePoint. My attention to detail and organisational skills have been consistently recognised by my line manager, and I'm often asked to quality check reports or help with new team member onboarding.

What I enjoy most is helping complex projects run smoothly behind the scenes. I take pride in noticing what's missing, filling gaps, and building structure around high-volume work. I've helped implement improvements to our grant claims process, created standard operating procedures, and simplified document templates to save time and reduce errors.

I'm excited by the opportunity to join the Civil Service at **HEO** level. I believe I could make a strong contribution in this role, not just because of my skills, but because I thrive in delivery-focused environments. I value structure, clarity, and professionalism — all of which I see reflected in this role and department. I'm particularly drawn to the variety the role offers and the chance to work across different teams, helping the organisation stay aligned and effective.

✦ Example 3: SEO – Project Manager (Approx. 900 words)

I currently work as a Programme Delivery Manager for a housing and regeneration consultancy, overseeing public-funded capital projects on behalf of local authority clients. I've worked in this role for three years and have a strong track record of leading delivery, managing partnerships, and producing high-quality reporting across complex programmes. My background spans project coordination, stakeholder engagement, and operational assurance, and I'm now keen to apply this experience within the Civil Service, particularly in a project delivery context with national impact.

In my current role, I manage a portfolio of infrastructure and regeneration projects, ranging from £500k to £5m in value. I coordinate regular client meetings, monitor delivery milestones, track spend and risk, and ensure that project information is submitted accurately and on time. I've led reporting and assurance work for projects that were later cited as examples of best practice by funding bodies, and I've supported procurement, contract mobilisation, and end-of-grant evaluations.

I regularly engage with senior local authority staff, contractors, and community representatives to resolve delivery issues and align expectations. I represent our organisation in stakeholder meetings, provide programme briefings, and escalate risks where required. I am confident using delivery plans, dashboards, and project documentation to support oversight and communicate progress effectively.

Alongside this, I support internal delivery improvement by streamlining how we gather and present data. I introduced a shared tracker that improved milestone visibility across teams and helped reduce last-minute reporting issues. I also helped develop a set of risk categories that made it easier for our junior staff to escalate early warning signs across projects.

I work well under pressure, manage competing deadlines confidently, and have developed a delivery-focused mindset that keeps both quality and timelines in balance. I enjoy working across teams and contributing to a culture of clarity, collaboration, and accountability. I've also supported recruitment and onboarding processes and provided informal coaching to colleagues new to project delivery.

I'm now looking to step into a Civil Service role where I can lead delivery while contributing to wider organisational goals. The **SEO** Project Manager role appeals to me because of its connection to place-based programmes, stakeholder accountability, and public outcomes. I'm confident I could bring immediate value to the team and would be keen to grow and contribute further through longer-term project cycles and collaboration with other departments.

✅ These statements:

- Mirror the job criteria from earlier in the book
- Show how applicants with no Civil Service background can clearly link their skills to the role
- Reflect the level of responsibility expected at **EO**, **HEO**, and **SEO**

✅ Final Tips

✅ DO:

- Refer to the job description and essential criteria
- Be clear and confident in tone
- Use examples, but don't just copy STAR behaviour content
- Show awareness of the department's work or values

❌ DON'T:

- Write a generic life story
- Repeat your CV word-for-word
- Forget to anonymise your statement
- Assume longer = better — it's the content that counts

Ready to start building your **behaviour statements** next?

In the next chapter, we'll look at how to use STAR effectively, how to avoid common pitfalls, and how to write examples that hit the mark for **EO**, **HEO**, and **SEO** roles.

Chapter 5: How to Write Behaviour Statements That Work

If there's one part of the Civil Service application that causes more frustration, confusion, and rejection than anything else — it's this.

Behaviour statements.

These short, 250-word examples are where a huge number of applicants fall down — not because they don't have the right experience, but because they don't know how to present it in the way the Civil Service expects.

You'll typically be given a behaviour (like **Making Effective Decisions** or **Delivering at Pace**) and asked to write an example showing how you've demonstrated that behaviour in a real-life situation.

Sounds straightforward — but the **sift is brutally competitive**, and assessors are trained to score strictly against the criteria. Many applications are rejected for reasons like:

- ✗ Not actually answering the behaviour (just describing duties)
- ✗ Writing too vaguely — or including too much irrelevant detail
- ✗ Focusing on the team's achievements instead of your own
- ✗ Using examples that don't match the grade level

And the worst part? Often the applicant never even knows why they were rejected — which makes it even more frustrating.

💡 The good news?

There's a way through this — and it's not about being flashy or having the "perfect" background. It's about learning to write clearly, confidently, and in a structure that assessors are trained to reward.

That structure is called **STAR** — and once you master it, you'll be ahead of most applicants straight away.

⭐ What Is STAR?

STAR is the most widely used method for structuring Civil Service behaviour examples — both in written applications and interviews.

It stands for:

- **Situation** – What was going on?

- **Task** – What needed to be done?
- **Action** – What *you* did (not your team)
- **Result** – What happened because of your actions?

Think of STAR like a mini story. Instead of listing skills or responsibilities, you're **showing** them — through a real example that follows a clear beginning, middle, and end.

💭 Why it matters:

- It helps the panel **see your thinking and decision-making in action**
- It makes your example **specific**, not generic
- It forces you to **focus on what *you* did**, not just what your team or organisation achieved

Even though STAR isn't unique to the Civil Service, it's **strongly encouraged in their guidance**, and panel members are trained to look for this kind of structured answer.

In fact, many candidate packs even mention it directly — especially for roles at EO, HEO and SEO level.

🎯 Your goal is to:

Use STAR to bring the behaviour to life — showing not just that you've done something before, but that you did it *well* and understood *why* it mattered.

We'll break down each part of the STAR model in the sections that follow.

🌑 S – Situation

This is your chance to **set the scene**. You don't need loads of detail — just enough for the reader to understand the context.

Think of it like the opening of a story. Answer questions like:

- Where were you working?
- What was the general setting or purpose of the work?
- Who else was involved (e.g. customers, team, managers)?
- Why was this situation significant?

💭 Tip: Keep it brief. You're not trying to impress them here — just give them a frame of reference.

Example:

I was working as part of a regional delivery team responsible for managing school infrastructure projects across the North West. Our team coordinated funding, timelines, and communication with academy trusts.

● T – Task

Now explain **what needed to be done**. What was your responsibility in the situation? What were you aiming to achieve?

This is not about what your *team* had to do — it's about **your goal or role within that situation**.

Answer:

- What was your objective or responsibility?
- Was there a specific problem or challenge to overcome?
- Were you expected to meet a deadline, target, or outcome?

💬 Tip: Keep this clear and focused — you're building up to the action next.

Example:

We were asked to investigate delays in a government-funded programme and provide a clear summary of issues and solutions to present at the upcoming programme board meeting.

● A – Action

This is the heart of your example — and the part where most people either **undersell themselves** or **drift into waffle**.

The Action section should focus on **you**. What steps did you take? What decisions did you make? What did you say, analyse, lead, improve, or manage?

This is where you:

- Show initiative
- Explain your thought process
- Demonstrate relevant behaviours (e.g. problem-solving, influencing, attention to detail)

Use **"I" statements**, not "we." Even if it was a team effort, the panel needs to know what *you* did.

🗨 Tip: If you're falling short of the word count, expand this section. That's where most marks come from.

Example:

I reviewed all project timelines to spot common delay points, then contacted 12 delivery partners to gather qualitative feedback. I noticed two key bottlenecks: unclear guidance and inconsistent approval times. I created a summary dashboard to visualise the delays, drafted suggested fixes, and shared it with my team lead before finalising our report.

R – Result

End with the outcome. What happened as a direct result of your actions?

This part is **brief but powerful** — and it's especially useful if you can quantify it (e.g. a percentage improvement, positive feedback, or process time saved).

Answer:

- What changed?
- Was the goal met?
- Did your actions make a difference?
- Did you learn something or improve a process for the future?

Even anecdotal results (like feedback from a manager or colleague) can be valuable if they show your impact.

Example:

The programme board approved our proposed changes, and within the next quarter, the average delay time dropped by 22%. I was commended by my manager for taking a clear, evidence-based approach and was asked to lead similar analysis work later that year.

💡 Why STAR Works

You might wonder:

"Do I really *have* to follow STAR? Can't I just write a good story in my own way?"

The truth is, you could — but unless you're an experienced writer with a deep understanding of Civil Service behaviours and grading expectations, **STAR gives you the best chance of success**.

Here's why it works so well — especially in competitive sift situations:

✅ It gives the panel a clear structure to follow

Civil Service sift panels often have **dozens or even hundreds of applications** to review — all under strict time and scoring guidance. A STAR-formatted response helps them quickly identify the key elements they're trained to assess: context, decision-making, personal contribution, and impact.

✅ It helps you stay focused

Without STAR, people tend to:

- Ramble or go off-topic
- Talk about what their team did rather than themselves
- Miss the actual behaviour being assessed

STAR forces you to focus on **a single moment**, which makes your answer sharper, more relevant, and easier to mark.

✅ It turns general duties into powerful evidence

Many applicants describe what their job involves — but not how they've applied that experience in action. STAR bridges that gap. It turns vague responsibilities into specific achievements.

✨ Instead of: "I deal with complaints daily."
You get: "I resolved a complex complaint by identifying the root cause, negotiating a solution, and reducing repeat issues by 30%."

✅ It gives you confidence at interview, too

Once you've written STAR-format behaviour statements, you'll find interviews much easier — because you already have your examples clearly structured in your mind. Many interview questions ask you to "tell me about a time when..." — which is STAR by design.

🎯 Bottom line?

STAR isn't about ticking boxes — it's about giving you a framework to tell your best stories with clarity, confidence, and impact.

⚠ Common Mistakes (And How to Fix Them)

Let's be honest — the majority of behaviour statements fall into the same traps. Here's what to avoid:

✖ Mistake 1: Listing Duties Instead of Giving an Example

Bad: "In my current role, I work with stakeholders and attend meetings to ensure things run smoothly."

✅ **Fix:** Show a **specific time** you influenced stakeholders and what changed as a result.

Better: "I led a cross-team meeting to resolve a disagreement between delivery leads, resulting in a revised project schedule being agreed and signed off."

✖ Mistake 2: Focusing Too Much on the Team

Bad: "We decided to review the process and agreed to implement changes."

✅ **Fix:** Show *your* role and impact. Even if it was collaborative, what did *you* bring to the table?

✖ Mistake 3: Writing Too Much or Too Little

250 words is tight — but try not to undershoot (e.g., 150 words) or massively overshoot. Keep it focused.

✅ **Tip:** Use around 1–2 sentences for Situation/Task, 3–5 for Action, and 1–2 for Result.

✎ How to Balance Your STAR

When writing your behaviour statement — especially with the 250-word limit in mind — a good rule of thumb is:

- **S – Situation:** ~10–15%
  Just set the scene quickly. Keep it brief.

- **T – Task:** ~10–15%
  Clarify what *you* were expected to do.

- **A – Action:** ~60–70%
  This is the **heart** of your example. Focus on *what you did*, how you approached it, what you considered, who you influenced, what steps you took, and how you adapted.

- **R – Result:** ~10–15%
  Keep it outcome-focused — ideally measurable or observable, even if just anecdotal.

✅ **Tip:** If you're struggling to hit the word count, expand the *Action* section. It's where most of your marks come from — especially when it comes to showing behaviours in action, decision-making, and personal impact.

📐 Tailoring to the Behaviour

STAR gives you the structure — but the **content** of your answer still needs to be shaped by the **specific behaviour** being assessed.

Each Civil Service behaviour is designed to test something different — so your STAR story should reflect the unique focus of that behaviour.

This is where many applicants go wrong. They use a decent example but fail to *show the right thing*. The panel isn't just marking the quality of your work — they're marking how well your example demonstrates the behaviour in question.

💬 Example: Making Effective Decisions

This behaviour is all about:

- Judgement
- Weighing up evidence
- Making sound, timely decisions
- Understanding risk and impact

A good STAR example for this should include:

- A situation where you had to evaluate different options
- What you considered before making your decision (e.g. time, risk, people)
- Why you chose one course of action over another
- What changed as a result of your decision

✅ **Panel tip:** They're looking for signs of logic, awareness, and accountability — not just instinct or "what felt right."

🗣 Example: Communicating and Influencing

This behaviour is about:

- Sharing ideas clearly and appropriately
- Understanding your audience
- Persuading or influencing others effectively

A good STAR example for this should include:

- **Who** you needed to influence or communicate with (e.g. a customer, colleague, senior manager)
- **How** you did it (e.g. email, in-person, presentation, report)
- **Why** you chose that method — and how you tailored it
- **What impact** your communication had (e.g. changed someone's mind, got something approved, reduced conflict)

📌 **Panel tip:** They're looking for evidence of *intentional* communication — not just that you passed on a message, but that you thought about *how* to do it effectively.

📌 **Key takeaway:**

A strong STAR story is one thing — but to score highly, it also needs to be the **right kind of story** for the behaviour you're being assessed on.

We'll go through detailed examples of each common behaviour later in the book — including ones tailored to EO, HEO, and SEO levels — so you can see how this comes to life.

🎯 **Tailoring to the Grade**

Here's one of the biggest hidden reasons why people fail the sift — even when their examples are decent:

❌ They're writing at the wrong level for the job.

The Civil Service often uses the **same behaviour headings** (like *Working Together* or *Delivering at Pace*) across multiple grades. But the level of **responsibility, complexity, and impact** expected increases as you move from EO to HEO to SEO.

That means your example might sound perfectly fine — but if it doesn't show enough ownership or decision-making for the grade you're applying for, it won't score highly.

Same Behaviour — Different Expectations

Let's look at how one behaviour (*Working Together*) might play out at different levels:

GRADE	WHAT YOU MIGHT SHOW
EO	Worked with a colleague to improve a shared process or resolve a simple issue.
HEO	Coordinated a task across teams or managed expectations between different stakeholders.
SEO	Influenced multiple senior stakeholders to align on a delivery strategy or resolve a cross-cutting issue.

☑ The difference isn't the topic — it's the **scale, ownership, and leadership** shown in the example.

🔍 Quick Self-Check:

Ask yourself:

- Did I **lead**, **coordinate**, or just **contribute**?
- Was I **responsible** for an outcome, or just helping someone else?
- Did my actions have a **wider impact** or involve working across teams or with senior stakeholders?

If your example sounds like something a junior colleague could do, it's probably **not right for SEO or HEO** — even if it's a well-written STAR.

📌 Final tip:

Tailor both your language *and* your content to the grade. Use words like "coordinated," "led," "negotiated," or "took ownership" when appropriate — they carry more weight than "helped" or "assisted."

You'll see this in action throughout the STAR examples later in the book.

📑 Examples

Now let's bring it to life with real STAR examples tailored to each grade level — so you can see exactly what a strong response looks like at **EO**, **HEO**, and **SEO**.

Delivering at Pace

Example Scenario

A project manager in a private sector firm is informed that a key client deliverable — the launch of a regional marketing campaign — must go live in just five working days, rather than the originally agreed ten. Failure to meet the new deadline would breach the client contract and risk losing future business. The manager must quickly replan the work, coordinate internal and external teams, and keep quality standards high despite the compressed timeline.

Executive Officer (EO) Level Example

S – Situation
I was working as a junior marketing assistant supporting a team delivering a regional campaign for a high-profile client. Midway through the project, we were told the launch date had been brought forward by five days due to changes in the client's availability.

T – Task
My manager asked me to take ownership of finalising and uploading the campaign content onto our platform — something I hadn't done before independently — and ensure it was client-ready within 48 hours.

A – Action
I reviewed the campaign assets against the checklist and highlighted a few that still needed input from our design team. I reached out to the designer, clearly flagged the new deadline, and negotiated a slot in their schedule. I then quality-checked the uploaded content against brand guidelines, and flagged one error which I corrected before final sign-off.

R – Result
The content went live on time, and the client fed back that the campaign was "slick and professional." My line manager commended my focus and attention to detail under pressure.

Higher Executive Officer (HEO) Level Example

S – Situation
While working as a project coordinator on a regional marketing launch, we were informed that the client needed the campaign to go live within five working days — half the time originally planned — due to a sudden shift in their product release schedule.

T – Task
I was responsible for re-scoping the delivery plan and coordinating our internal content,

design, and analytics teams to meet the new launch deadline without compromising on quality.

A – Action
I ran an emergency planning meeting that afternoon to reallocate tasks and fast-track dependencies. I negotiated shorter review times from the creative lead and introduced twice-daily stand-up calls to keep the team aligned. I also managed expectations with the client, agreeing to stagger the campaign rollout slightly while maintaining their key launch window.

R – Result
The campaign launched within the new timeframe, and the client was satisfied with both the outcome and our responsiveness. The head of marketing asked me to lead the next phase of delivery based on how well I'd handled the compressed deadline.

Senior Executive Officer (SEO) Level Example

S – Situation
As the project manager for a strategic regional campaign, I was informed that the client's executive board had moved the go-live date forward by five working days to align with a national announcement — creating significant delivery risk.

T – Task
I was accountable for the successful launch of the campaign within the new deadline. This required urgent reprioritisation of internal resources, contract renegotiations with external suppliers, and direct engagement with the client's leadership team to manage expectations.

A – Action
Within hours, I held a risk-assessment meeting with senior stakeholders, identified critical path elements, and suspended lower-priority activities. I negotiated a reduced turnaround time with our external agency while maintaining legal sign-off procedures. I also briefed the client's communications director personally to explain the revised delivery approach and secured agreement on phased deliverables. Internally, I delegated technical QA ownership to a trusted team lead and focused on tracking executive-level risks.

R – Result
The campaign launched on time, in line with the client's high-visibility announcement. We avoided any reputational or contractual fallout, and I received direct thanks from the client's director for my strategic handling of the situation. My delivery model was shared across other accounts facing time-sensitive launches.

◆ Communicating and Influencing

Example Scenario

The organisation is rolling out a new internal case management system. Some staff are resistant to the change — worried about the extra workload, confused about the benefits, or disengaged due to poor past experiences with new systems. The candidate must adapt their communication approach to win buy-in, reduce resistance, and help ensure the new system is successfully adopted.

Executive Officer (EO) Level Example

S – Situation
As an admin officer in a local housing association, I was supporting the rollout of a new case management system across the admin and support teams. Some colleagues were openly frustrated about the change, expressing concerns that it would slow down their work or cause issues with client records.

T – Task
I was asked to support the transition by helping my team get comfortable with the system and encourage them to use it properly during the pilot phase.

A – Action
I set up short lunchtime drop-in sessions where colleagues could ask questions informally. I also created a simple one-page guide with the key steps they needed to follow, using plain language and screenshots. When one colleague expressed concern in a team meeting, I spoke to them privately afterwards to better understand their worries and reassured them based on what I'd learned during training.

R – Result
Colleagues began using the new system more confidently, and attendance at my drop-ins increased each day. My manager said the team's transition was smoother than expected and credited the informal support sessions I'd put in place.

Higher Executive Officer (HEO) Level Example

S – Situation
As a project officer overseeing the rollout of a new case management system in a regional charity, I noticed resistance from several staff — especially team leads who felt the rollout was rushed and feared loss of productivity during the changeover.

T – Task
I was responsible for improving engagement and encouraging staff to adopt the new system in line with our project timeline.

A – Action
I arranged short, tailored briefings for different teams, adapting the message depending on their role and how the system would affect their workflow. I shared real examples of time saved during pilot testing, and highlighted how the system could reduce manual errors — one of their key frustrations. I also created an FAQ document addressing the concerns raised in earlier feedback sessions and made sure team leads had a dedicated contact person for follow-up questions.

R – Result
Adoption rates improved within two weeks, and one of the previously sceptical teams became an internal advocate for the new system. My manager highlighted my communication strategy in the post-implementation review, noting it reduced transition issues by over 30% compared to previous rollouts.

● Senior Executive Officer (SEO) Level Example

S – Situation
In my role as **SEO** programme lead in a national support charity, I was overseeing a large-scale digital transformation project. The new case management system would impact over 100 staff across multiple regions, and there was significant pushback from senior stakeholders concerned about disruption, data integrity, and the lack of capacity for additional training.

T – Task
I was responsible for ensuring that stakeholders across all levels — from frontline staff to regional directors — understood the purpose of the change, felt heard, and were willing to support the rollout.

A – Action
I developed a tiered communications strategy, starting with early engagement sessions for regional leads to address strategic concerns and gain early support. I briefed each leadership group with tailored talking points so they could cascade the messaging in a consistent, confident way. I also recorded a short video explainer with key FAQs and success metrics, which was shared network-wide. To address frontline concerns, I invited a pilot team lead to present their positive experience at a national all-staff webinar, reinforcing trust through peer-to-peer communication.

R – Result
Buy-in from senior stakeholders improved significantly, with 90% attending follow-up planning meetings. System adoption targets were met ahead of schedule, and post-launch feedback noted the clarity and accessibility of the communications strategy as a key success factor.

Making Effective Decisions

Example Scenario

The candidate works in a role where they're presented with multiple options, each with pros and cons, and they must make a reasoned decision under time or operational pressure. They consider evidence, risks, and impacts — and explain how they reached their choice.

The scenario involves managing a conflicting set of requests for limited resources (e.g., staffing or funding), requiring the candidate to balance competing priorities and justify their decision.

This is a great behaviour for showing:

- Sound judgement
- Structured thinking
- Accountability
- Confidence in decision-making — even when not everyone agrees

---

Executive Officer (EO) Level Example

S – Situation
As a rota coordinator in a residential care service, I received a request from two team leads asking for the same staff member to be assigned to their shift on a bank holiday. Only one request could be honoured.

T – Task
I was responsible for allocating staff fairly while ensuring that each shift had the right level of cover based on resident needs.

A – Action
I reviewed both shift plans and checked the complexity of care needs for each. One team had more critical care requirements, while the other had less dependency. I then checked with the staff member if they had a preference, which they didn't. I documented my decision rationale and assigned the staff member to the higher-need shift. I informed both leads with a short email explaining the factors I considered and offered to support the other team with a quick rota shuffle to help cover their less urgent tasks.

R – Result
Both teams accepted the decision, and care delivery was unaffected. My line manager later noted that I'd handled the situation with maturity and fairness, especially given the short notice.

● Higher Executive Officer (HEO) Level Example

S – Situation
While working in a grant administration team, I received two competing funding requests for urgent school repairs — both valid, but our regional pot could only support one during the current quarter.

T – Task
I had to assess both cases, make a recommendation for allocation, and present a clear rationale to senior colleagues and the applicants.

A – Action
I reviewed each application against our funding criteria, then looked at risk and urgency: one school had minor roof damage, while the other reported heating failure ahead of winter. I contacted both schools to validate the information and gathered photos and impact statements. I also looked at delivery timelines to ensure the money could be spent in time. I documented the analysis in a short briefing note, outlining my recommendation and offering a timeline for reconsidering the second request in the next round.

R – Result
My recommendation was approved, and the heating repair was funded and completed ahead of the cold weather. The other applicant thanked us for the transparency, and I was later asked to lead a refresher session for new team members on handling competing bids.

● Senior Executive Officer (SEO) Level Example

S – Situation
As an **SEO** in a policy delivery team, I was overseeing the rollout of an emergency education recovery fund. Midway through the planning stage, new data suggested that a key region needed significantly more support — but our national budget could not be adjusted without delaying the entire programme.

T – Task
I had to decide whether to reallocate funding internally — risking dissatisfaction in other regions — or proceed with the original allocations and delay extra support for the high-need area.

A – Action
I convened a rapid data review with our analysts and regional advisors to validate the new need. I then modelled three scenarios, assessing reputational risk, delivery timelines, and equity of access. I shared my options with our G7 lead and proposed a hybrid solution: a small internal reallocation from regions with slower spend profiles, paired with a public commitment to top-up funding next quarter. I also drafted the comms plan to explain the reasoning and manage expectations across stakeholders.

R – Result

The adjusted plan was signed off within 48 hours. The high-need region received the urgent support they required, and the overall programme remained on track. My approach was later referenced in a departmental review as an example of pragmatic decision-making under pressure.

◆ Working Together

💬 Example Scenario

The candidate is part of a cross-functional team working on a time-sensitive project (e.g., organising an event, launching a campaign, or resolving a service delivery issue). The project faces collaboration challenges — such as unclear responsibilities, personality clashes, or competing priorities. The candidate plays a key role in bringing people together, improving cooperation, and keeping the project on track.

This scenario is great for demonstrating:

- Relationship-building
- Conflict resolution
- Team awareness
- Clear, respectful communication
- Collective success over individual contribution

● Executive Officer (EO) Level Example

S – Situation
As a support officer in a local council team delivering a public awareness event, I noticed tensions between our design and admin teams — each blaming the other for delays in preparing event materials.

T – Task
Although not in a leadership role, I took it upon myself to improve communication between both teams so we could get the materials finalised before the print deadline.

A – Action
I spoke separately with the team leads to understand the issues. I learned that both groups were waiting on different approvals but hadn't clarified expectations. I created a shared tracker so everyone could see the status of tasks, and suggested a short daily check-in to avoid miscommunication. I also helped draft clearer guidance on what each team needed to sign off.

R – Result
Tension eased quickly, the materials were delivered on time, and both teams thanked me for stepping in. My line manager said my proactive attitude had helped avoid a potentially embarrassing delay.

● Higher Executive Officer (HEO) Level Example

S – Situation
While coordinating a regional careers fair involving multiple local authorities and private sponsors, I noticed poor engagement in planning meetings — tasks weren't being picked up, and deadlines were slipping.

T – Task
As the main organiser, I needed to improve collaboration between stakeholders and get planning back on track without causing conflict.

A – Action
I set up a planning workshop focused on shared goals and created a visual timeline showing how delays would impact each party. I assigned clear roles based on people's strengths and sent a follow-up action plan with named responsibilities. I also offered one-to-one support to two quieter members who'd felt sidelined in previous meetings.

R – Result
The event was fully staffed and launched on schedule, with positive feedback from attendees and stakeholders. Several partners said the collaborative approach made them more open to working together on future events.

● Senior Executive Officer (SEO) Level Example

S – Situation
As **SEO** lead on a national project involving multiple delivery partners, I inherited a team with visible tension — one key partner felt their input was being ignored, and communications between them and my team had broken down.

T – Task
I needed to rebuild trust, re-establish effective communication, and create a shared working model that would get the project back on track.

A – Action
I scheduled a roundtable session where both teams could raise concerns openly. I acknowledged the issues and facilitated a neutral conversation focused on shared outcomes. I proposed a new governance model with clearly defined roles, escalation routes, and joint decision checkpoints. I followed up with a summary note, ensuring everyone agreed on next steps. I also nominated a senior liaison from each organisation to keep dialogue open going forward.

R – Result

The working relationship improved significantly, and joint milestone reporting resumed within two weeks. The project was delivered successfully, and feedback from both organisations highlighted the inclusive approach and improved trust.

Other Behaviours You Might Encounter

While most Civil Service roles — especially at EO, HEO and SEO level — tend to focus on a core set of behaviours (like **Communicating and Influencing**, **Working Together**, and **Delivering at Pace**), there are a few others that may pop up depending on the nature of the role or the department you're applying to.

These **less common behaviours** might not appear in every application, but it's important to know what they mean — especially if you're applying for:

- A **policy, project delivery**, or **operational management** role
- A role in a **specialist team** (e.g. strategy, performance, regulation, digital, etc.)
- Or you're applying for a promotion or moving toward **leadership** responsibility

---

Why they're less common (but still important)

These behaviours are assessed **less frequently at EO–SEO** level because many entry- and mid-level roles are focused more on delivery and collaboration than high-level decision-making or strategic leadership.

However, when they **do appear**, they usually signal one of two things:

1. The role carries more **autonomy, oversight**, or **responsibility** than usual
2. The department is looking for candidates who can **grow into leadership or policy roles** in the future

That's why it's worth being prepared — even if your immediate job doesn't require full leadership responsibilities, showing early potential can still score well.

Where these behaviours might appear

You're more likely to encounter behaviours like **Making Effective Decisions, Leadership**, or **Managing a Quality Service** if:

- You're applying for an **SEO role**
- The role involves **line management, leading a process**, or **stakeholder engagement**

- You'll be making **judgements, prioritising workloads**, or **representing the department** externally
- The department is **delivery-focused** and values operational performance or measurable results

You may also see them pop up in:

- **Band A or Band B** roles in devolved governments (e.g. Scottish Government or Welsh Government)
- **Project roles** that require analytical or risk-based decision-making
- **Jobs that act as a stepping stone to G7 or beyond**

📌 What this section is for:

This section isn't about memorising policy definitions — it's about giving you the **confidence to recognise** these behaviours when they show up, and the tools to respond with relevant, structured examples.

Even a basic understanding of what each behaviour looks like in practice will put you ahead of applicants who treat it like a guessing game.

◆ Leadership

👥 Behaviour Summary

Leadership isn't just about managing people — it's about setting direction, motivating others, taking accountability, and creating an environment where people can do their best work. Even without formal authority, leadership can be demonstrated through ownership and influence.

✨ HEO-Level STAR Example

S – Situation
While coordinating a department-wide onboarding review, I noticed that new joiners were consistently raising the same issues about unclear guidance and inconsistent IT setup during their first week.

T – Task
I volunteered to lead a small working group to improve the onboarding experience, even though I didn't have formal management responsibilities.

A – Action
I brought together colleagues from HR, IT, and each business unit to identify what was

and wasn't working. I encouraged open discussion and made sure everyone's suggestions were documented. I then drafted a revised onboarding checklist, aligned tasks to owners, and created a two-page welcome guide for managers to support new starters. I also presented the proposal to senior management and incorporated their feedback before rollout.

R – Result

The changes were introduced the following quarter and new joiner satisfaction scores improved by 40%. I was recognised at the quarterly all-staff meeting for leading the initiative with confidence and inclusivity.

● EO-Level Comparison Note:

At **EO**, leadership might look like:

- Volunteering to lead a small task or process
- Helping onboard a new colleague
- Supporting others through change or uncertainty
- Taking responsibility when no one else has stepped up

The emphasis is on **personal responsibility and informal influence**.

● SEO-Level Comparison Note:

At **SEO**, leadership involves:

- Driving delivery through others
- Holding people to account for performance
- Managing competing priorities and conflicting views
- Shaping team culture or vision

It's about **strategic direction, credibility, and accountability** — especially when leading across teams or working under pressure.

◆ Managing a Quality Service

Behaviour Summary

This behaviour focuses on delivering consistent, effective, and high-quality services — whether to internal colleagues, partner organisations, or the public.

✨ HEO-Level STAR Example

S – Situation
While managing a regional inbox for school funding queries, I noticed that response times were inconsistent and queries were often forwarded multiple times before reaching the right person.

T – Task
I was asked to review the inbox handling process to improve response times and reduce duplication.

A – Action
I analysed common queries and mapped out which team should handle each type. I introduced a simple tagging system and drafted a referral guide to help colleagues triage messages faster. I also created an auto-response with updated contact info for key services and offered refresher training to newer staff.

R – Result
The average response time dropped by 35%, and satisfaction feedback from stakeholders improved. My guidance was later shared with another region facing similar issues.

● EO-Level Comparison Note:

At **EO**, this could involve:

- Following processes accurately to ensure good service
- Spotting a small issue and raising it with a supervisor
- Taking extra care to handle a customer query properly

It's about **maintaining quality and doing the basics really well.**

● SEO-Level Comparison Note:

At **SEO**, this behaviour might include:

- Overseeing service delivery at scale

- Holding others accountable for standards
- Making improvements based on service feedback
- Managing risks that affect the service

You're expected to **shape, lead, and monitor service quality**, not just deliver it.

◆ Seeing the Bigger Picture

Behaviour Summary

This behaviour is about understanding how your work fits into broader priorities — whether at team, organisation, or national level. It includes strategic awareness, understanding impact, and spotting future implications.

HEO-Level STAR Example

S – Situation
While contributing to a report on regional school building performance, I realised that the way we were presenting data didn't clearly show how it linked to national sustainability targets.

T – Task
I suggested re-framing the reporting section so that it more clearly aligned with government priorities, helping senior leaders understand progress in context.

A – Action
I reviewed the department's sustainability strategy and pulled out key targets relevant to our region. I worked with our analysts to repackage the data in a visual format and included a short narrative explaining how local projects supported the wider aims. I also included a suggestion for a new KPI to track carbon reduction from retrofit projects.

R – Result
The updated report was praised by the deputy director and was used in a briefing to the minister. Our region was also asked to present our reporting approach at a national forum.

EO-Level Comparison Note:

At **EO**, this behaviour might involve:

- Asking why a task is needed and how it helps
- Showing interest in wider team goals
- Being aware of how your actions affect others

It's about **awareness of purpose**, even if you're not shaping strategy.

● SEO-Level Comparison Note:

At **SEO**, this could involve:

- Translating high-level strategy into operational plans
- Spotting risks or trends before they escalate
- Representing your team's work in cross-government conversations
- Shaping direction based on political or policy shifts

This level is about **strategic thinking and alignment** across teams or programmes.

◆ Changing and Improving

Behaviour Summary

This behaviour is about finding better ways to do things. It's not just about innovation — it's about showing awareness of problems or inefficiencies, suggesting improvements, and helping to implement them. At higher grades, it also involves influencing others to embrace change.

HEO-Level STAR Example

S – Situation
While working in a grant administration team, I noticed that our internal process for recording project updates from applicants was inconsistent and often duplicated across spreadsheets, which led to delays and confusion during quarterly reviews.

T – Task
I took the lead in reviewing the process to see if we could reduce duplication and make it easier to track updates in real time.

A – Action
I met with colleagues across the team to understand their current workflows and pain points. I mapped out the common data points and proposed moving to a shared online form that would automatically feed into a central tracker. I tested the new approach with a small group of users, gathered feedback, and made adjustments to improve usability. I then created a short guide and ran a demo session to support the wider rollout.

R – Result
The new system reduced duplication by over 40% and improved accuracy in reporting.

Feedback from the team was positive, and it was adopted as the new standard approach. My line manager noted that the change significantly improved our efficiency during reporting cycles.

🔵 EO-Level Comparison Note:

At **EO** level, Changing and Improving might look like:

- Suggesting a small improvement to a task you regularly perform
- Adapting an existing process to save time or reduce errors
- Testing and suggesting a better template or form based on your day-to-day experience

The focus is usually on **your own work** area and taking initiative in a limited scope.

🔵 SEO-Level Comparison Note:

At **SEO** level, the behaviour typically involves:

- Leading a change across multiple teams or functions
- Securing stakeholder buy-in for new processes
- Managing risk while implementing improvements on a larger scale
- Embedding continuous improvement into team culture

The emphasis shifts from "making a helpful tweak" to **driving sustained, strategic change**.

♦ Changing and Improving

🏆 Behaviour Summary

This behaviour is about supporting learning and growth — in yourself and in others. It includes coaching, knowledge sharing, personal reflection, and helping others improve.

✨ HEO-Level STAR Example

S – Situation
After attending training on a new digital tool used for risk assessments, I noticed that several colleagues were still struggling to use it confidently, which delayed our monthly reporting.

T – Task

Although I wasn't a formal trainer, I took it upon myself to support the team's learning and speed up adoption.

A – Action

I created a short guide with screenshots and tips based on common issues I'd seen. I offered optional lunchtime "quick tips" sessions for anyone who wanted support. I also stayed behind after a team meeting to help one colleague 1:1 and tailored my explanation to their role.

R – Result

Within two weeks, the team's reporting time dropped by 20%, and the accuracy of submissions improved. Colleagues began referring others to me for help, and my manager thanked me for supporting the wider team's development without being asked.

EO-Level Comparison Note:

At **EO**, this behaviour could involve:

- Sharing a useful tip with a colleague
- Offering to help someone learn a system or process
- Asking for feedback and applying it

The focus is on learning from and supporting peers, not formal development planning.

SEO-Level Comparison Note:

At **SEO**, this behaviour might look like:

- Coaching staff or peers
- Building development into team objectives
- Creating a culture of feedback and improvement
- Supporting capability growth across a wider function

This level is about actively investing in growth — both strategically and practically.

Chapter 6: Mastering the Sift Stage

So, you've written your behaviour statements. You've followed the STAR format. You've hit the word count. But then... silence. Or worse — the dreaded *"Unfortunately, you have not been successful at this stage."*

What happened?

This chapter explains what the sift is, how your application is assessed, and why even strong candidates often get sifted out. More importantly, it shows how to avoid the most common mistakes and give yourself the best chance of success.

What Is the Sift Stage?

The sift is the stage where your written application is reviewed by a panel. For most **EO–SEO** roles, this happens **before** the interview and determines whether you progress to the next stage.

At sift, you're assessed almost entirely on your **behaviour statements** (and sometimes a personal statement). The sift panel is checking to see if your examples show the behaviour at the right level for the job.

It's not about personality. It's not about potential. It's about evidence — have you demonstrated the required behaviours clearly and confidently?

Who Assesses Your Application?

Your application is reviewed by a **panel of trained Civil Servants**, usually at the same or higher grade than the role you're applying for. Each panel member independently reviews your behaviour statements using a **scoring framework**, then scores are moderated and agreed.

Most departments use a **1 to 7 scale**, with the following rough breakdown:

SCORE	MEANING
1–2	Weak – Little or no evidence of the behaviour
3	Limited – Partially relevant or unclear
4	Acceptable – Meets the basic standard at the grade level (often the minimum passing score)
5	Strong – Clear, structured, and well-evidenced
6–7	Excellent – High-quality and above-grade performance (rare)

Note: Not all departments share scores with candidates — but many do include them in your application feedback after the sift.

Tip: Scoring a 5 or above is rare. Many successful applicants score 4s across the board and still progress to interview.

What Are They Looking For?

At sift, the panel is looking for three things in every behaviour answer:

1. **Relevance** – Does it directly address the behaviour being tested?
2. **Structure** – Is it written clearly using STAR, with logical flow?
3. **Grade Fit** – Is the example appropriate for the level (**EO**, **HEO**, or **SEO**)?

You might have done a great job in real life — but if it's not communicated effectively, you won't get the marks.

Why Good Candidates Fail the Sift

1. Listing Duties Instead of Giving a Real Example

"In my current role, I manage a team, work with others, and communicate regularly."

Fix: Turn it into a story. Pick a real situation and use STAR to bring it to life.

---

2. Giving the Wrong Level of Example

A candidate applying for **SEO** gives an example of helping a colleague one-on-one — which is more suited to **EO**.

Fix: Check your example matches the grade expectations — use the examples earlier in this book as a guide.

---

3. Trying to Cram in Too Much

"This is when I showed leadership, teamwork, decision-making, and influencing…"

Fix: Focus on one behaviour per answer. Go deep, not wide.

✘ 4. Being Too Vague

"We worked together to improve the process, and it worked well."

✅ Fix: Add detail. What exactly did you do? How did it improve things? What changed?

✘ 5. Forgetting to Show the Result

The STAR ends with the action… and no outcome.

✅ Fix: Even if there wasn't a dramatic result, always close with the impact — even if it's "my manager praised me" or "it prevented a delay."

📋 Checklist Before You Submit

Use this mini checklist before hitting "submit":

- ✅ Have I followed the STAR structure?
- ✅ Did I focus on one clear behaviour per answer?
- ✅ Did I show my personal contribution (not just the team)?
- ✅ Does the example match the grade I'm applying for?
- ✅ Did I include a result or outcome?

If the answer is "yes" to all of the above, you're in a much stronger position than most applicants.

✅ In Summary

- **The sift is about showing *evidence* — not effort.**
- **Use STAR for structure, focus on the Action, and show impact.**
- **Avoid vague or low-level examples. Match the behaviour *and* the grade.**
- **Strong, clear writing at this stage is what gets you through to interview — not your potential, your passion, or your personality (that comes next).**

If your behaviour statements do their job, you'll clear the sift and be invited to interview — and that's where the real test begins. Let's look at how to prepare for the next stage with confidence.

🎤 Chapter 7: Nailing the Interview Stage

Congratulations — You've successfully reached the interview!

You've successfully made it through the sift — which means your behaviour examples, CV, or personal statement showed the panel that you're a credible candidate.

Now, it's time to **face the interview panel**.

For many applicants, this is the most daunting part of the process. You might worry about nerves, going blank, or not knowing what they'll ask.

But here's the good news:

☑ **Civil Service interviews are structured, predictable, and learnable.**

They're not like free-flowing private sector interviews where you're judged on personality or chemistry. Civil Service panels use a **clear marking framework**, based on the Success Profiles you've already encountered in the application.

If you've made it this far, you've already got what it takes to do well. Now it's about understanding how the interview works — and learning how to present yourself clearly, confidently, and in a way that matches what the panel is looking for.

🍱 What This Chapter Covers:

In this chapter, we'll walk you through:

- 🧱 The structure of a Civil Service interview
- 🎯 What's assessed (and how)
- 🔄 How expectations change between grades (EO, HEO, SEO)
- 💬 How to prepare for **behaviours** and **strengths** questions
- 💡 Practical tips to improve your confidence, timing, and performance

Whether this is your first ever interview — or just your first *Civil Service* interview — this chapter is here to take the guesswork out of it.

🧱 What Is a Civil Service Interview Like?

Most Civil Service interviews follow the **Success Profiles framework** — the same one used in the application stage.

That means you're not going to be asked trick questions or put on the spot in an aggressive way. Instead, the panel will ask you a series of clear, focused questions that assess your ability to do the job based on:

- ☑ **Behaviours** (your past actions in specific situations)
- ☑ **Strengths** (what energises you — and how you naturally work)
- 🔲 Occasionally: **Experience, Technical Skills,** or **Ability**
  (These are more common in specialist roles, fast stream, or grades above SEO.)

👥 Who's on the panel?

You'll typically be interviewed by **a panel of 2–3 trained assessors**. This might include:

- A manager from the team you're applying to join
- An independent panel member (to ensure fairness and consistency)
- A Civil Service HR or recruitment rep

They're not there to catch you out. Their job is to:

- Ask standardised questions
- Score your answers against a clear benchmark
- Treat every candidate fairly and consistently

The same question is usually asked to **every applicant** — and scored using a structured 1–7 scale, just like the sift.

🧠 Why this matters:

Knowing how Civil Service interviews work takes the pressure off. You don't have to be perfect — you just have to be:

- Clear
- Focused
- And aligned with the behaviours and strengths the job is looking for

This is a **performance-based interview**, not a personality contest.

🧠 How Are You Assessed?

Civil Service interviews are not about "gut feeling" or whether the panel likes you — they're assessed using a structured, fair scoring system.

Each question you're asked is scored **individually**, based on how well your answer demonstrates the behaviour or strength being assessed.

The scoring is usually done on a **1 to 7 scale**, with each number linked to a set of criteria. For example:

SCORE	WHAT IT MEANS
1–2	Very little evidence — didn't meet the mark
3–4	Some evidence — but weak or incomplete
5–6	Strong evidence — good detail and relevance
7	Excellent evidence — directly meets all criteria at the right level

So if your answer is vague, too short, or focused on the team rather than your personal contribution, you might only score a 3 or 4. But if it's structured, specific, and focused on what *you* did, you're far more likely to hit 6 or 7.

🎯 Key Difference from the Sift:

At sift stage, the panel is reading your written answers — and giving you a score based on what's on the page.

At interview, they're also assessing:

- **How clearly you explain yourself**
- **Whether you come across as confident and self-aware**
- **Whether your examples hold up under gentle follow-up questions**

That's why it's so important to **practice speaking your answers out loud**. The content is still key — but your tone, clarity, and structure all make a difference.

🚀 **Good news:** If you've made it to interview, it means your written application showed potential. Now your job is to **back it up verbally** — with the same STAR examples, but spoken clearly and confidently.

📝 Interview Format

Most Civil Service interviews at **EO, HEO, and SEO level** follow a fairly consistent format — and that's great news for you. The more predictable the structure, the easier it is to prepare effectively.

Here's what you can usually expect:

✅ Behaviour Questions (3 to 5)

These are the **core** of the interview. You'll be asked to provide real-life examples that demonstrate specific Civil Service behaviours (e.g. *Working Together, Communicating and Influencing, Making Effective Decisions*).

You'll use the **STAR method** to structure your answers — just like you did in your written application.

- 🕐 Plan to speak for around **3–4 minutes per behaviour**
- 💬 These are scored on the **same 1–7 scale** as the sift

✅ Strengths Questions (2 to 3)

These are quicker, less structured questions that explore your **natural preferences and working style**. There's no STAR format here — the focus is on **authenticity, positivity, and alignment with the role**.

You'll usually answer these in **1–2 minutes** per question.

💡 Additional Tasks (if applicable)

Some interviews may include a **task or exercise** before or after the main questions. This will always be listed in the job advert or candidate pack.

You might be asked to complete:

- 📊 A short **presentation** (you'll be told the topic in advance)
- 📝 A **written exercise** (e.g. analysing information, drafting an email)
- 📁 A **case study** (e.g. prioritising tasks, making a recommendation)

🔍 These are used to assess specific strengths, communication, judgement, or your ability to work under pressure

---

🎯 Virtual vs In-Person Interviews

Most interviews are now conducted **virtually via Microsoft Teams**, though some departments still offer face-to-face options.

If your interview is virtual:

- You can use **notes** or **bullet points** — but try not to read word-for-word
- Check your tech in advance: connection, camera, microphone

- Keep eye contact by glancing at the camera when speaking
- Make sure your background is quiet and neutral if possible

Knowing the format in advance means you can **plan, prepare, and practice** — and walk in (or log in!) with confidence.

🗣 Behaviour Questions (STAR Method Still Applies)

Behaviour questions are the **heart of a Civil Service interview** — and the most important part to prepare for.

These questions are designed to test how well you've demonstrated specific behaviours in the past. You'll recognise them because they almost always start with:

- "Tell us about a time when…"
- "Describe a situation where…"
- "Give an example of how you…"

These are your **cue to use STAR** — and your chance to show the panel how you think, act, and take responsibility.

🔲 STAR Structure Still Applies

Just like in your written application, the STAR method is your go-to structure:

- **S – Situation** (what was going on?)
- **T – Task** (what needed to be done?)
- **A – Action** (what did *you* do?)
- **R – Result** (what happened?)

The biggest difference is that you're now saying it out loud — and you have **3 to 4 minutes** to deliver each answer clearly and confidently.

🎤 How to Handle Behaviour Questions in Real Time

1. **Start with a 1-line summary**
   This helps you stay on track and gives the panel a quick overview.

"I'd like to talk about a time I managed a last-minute schedule change while supporting a team of five."

2. **Stick to the structure — but sound natural**
   You don't need to announce "S, T, A, R" out loud — just follow the flow behind the scenes. Speak in full sentences, and imagine you're telling the story to a colleague or mentor.

3. **Focus on the Action section**
   Most of your marks will come from this part. Talk clearly about what *you* did, what decisions you made, and how you responded to challenges. Use "I" more than "we."

4. **Land the Result with confidence**
   Don't forget to include the outcome — even if it's small. It helps the panel see the impact of your actions and closes the loop.

⏱ Timing Tip:

Aim for **1 sentence for Situation and Task each**, **4–5 sentences for Action**, and **1–2 for Result**.
Total: Around **3–4 minutes per question** is the sweet spot.

Good news: The panel *wants* you to succeed. They're not there to interrogate you — they're listening for evidence that you've demonstrated the behaviour well, at the right level.

How to Prepare for Behaviour Questions

The best way to feel confident in a Civil Service interview is to **prepare intentionally** — not just by reading your old behaviour examples, but by learning how to *talk through them naturally*.

Unlike the written stage, this part is about **delivery** as well as content. Strong preparation helps you sound focused, relaxed, and in control.

✅ 1. Revisit the behaviours in the job advert

Go back to the vacancy listing and look at the behaviours listed — these are almost always what the panel will ask you about.

If the advert lists:

- *Delivering at Pace*
- *Making Effective Decisions*

- *Working Together*
  ...those are the exact behaviours you'll need examples for.

Don't just Google generic examples — pick stories from your own experience.

---

2. Prepare 2 examples per behaviour

Why two?

Because:

- The panel may ask follow-up questions like "Can you give us another example?"
- Your first example might not be suitable once they finish reading the full question
- Having a backup gives you confidence and flexibility on the day

Example bank idea: Create a simple document or notes file with:

- 2 x Delivering at Pace examples
- 2 x Communicating and Influencing examples
- 2 x Working Together examples
  ...and so on.

---

3. Practice saying them aloud — with a timer

Speaking STAR examples out loud is **very different** from reading them on paper. Your tone, pace, and clarity all matter.

Try this:

- Use a **3–4 minute timer** to rehearse each example
- Record yourself or ask a friend to listen
- Focus on the **Action** section — that's where most marks are scored
- Practice transitions: "So what I did was..." or "The key step I took was..."

The goal isn't to memorise — it's to sound confident and fluent.

---

4. Start with a one-line summary

This helps you stay focused and helps the panel orient themselves to your story.

"I'd like to talk about a time I managed a service disruption that affected customer access to our online portal."

It gives you momentum — and gives the panel clarity straight away.

Strengths Questions: What Are They?

Strengths questions are the part of the interview most applicants overlook — but they're just as important to get right.

Unlike behaviour questions (which focus on *what you've done*), strengths questions are designed to explore:

- **What comes naturally to you**
- **What energises or motivates you**
- **Whether you're a good fit for the role and the team**

There's no STAR structure here. The panel isn't looking for long, detailed examples — they're listening for **authenticity, enthusiasm**, and a sense of **how you like to work**.

What Do These Questions Sound Like?

Strengths questions are often phrased like:

- "What does a good day at work look like for you?"
- "Do you prefer starting tasks or finishing them?"
- "How do you approach change?"
- "What motivates you in a team setting?"
- "Do you enjoy solving problems for others?"

They're quick-fire, personal, and not based on scoring factual accuracy. Instead, you're scored on:

- ✅ Whether your answer sounds **natural and authentic**
- ✅ Whether your strengths seem to **align with the role**
- ✅ Whether you bring a **positive and self-aware tone**

What Are the Panel Looking For?

The panel wants to see:

- That you understand your own preferences and motivations
- That you speak about them with **genuine energy**

- That your natural strengths suit the environment and responsibilities of the role

They're *not* expecting you to say what you think they want to hear. In fact, trying to sound too rehearsed or artificial can work against you.

📌 Your goal:

Sound confident, motivated, and self-aware — like someone who has thought about how they work best, and wants to bring that into a meaningful role.

💬 How to Prepare for Strengths Questions

Unlike behaviour questions, **you can't rehearse Strengths questions word-for-word** — and that's by design. They're meant to be spontaneous, personal, and authentic.

But that doesn't mean you can't prepare.

Here's how to get yourself into the right mindset — and make sure your answers hit the mark on the day.

✅ 1. Reflect on what energises you

Think about:

- The parts of your work you naturally enjoy
- The kinds of tasks that give you satisfaction
- How you like to approach challenges or pressure
- When you feel most motivated or in flow

💡 *Tip:* Strengths often tie into **how** you do things — not just what you do. Do you like planning? Bringing structure? Supporting others? Solving puzzles? Being efficient?

✅ 2. Know what the role values

Strengths questions aren't marked with a fixed scoring sheet — but the panel will be listening for **alignment with the job**.

If you're applying for a role that involves teamwork, fast-moving tasks, or dealing with the public, they'll expect to hear strengths that reflect that (e.g. empathy, resilience, flexibility).

❌ Saying "I enjoy working alone and being left to my own devices" might be true — but it won't help if the job involves collaboration and flexibility.

✅ 3. Speak naturally — not like a robot

The biggest trap people fall into is trying to sound "perfect" or memorised. That's not what the panel wants.

🎯 Instead, aim for **a natural, conversational tone** — like how you'd explain yourself to a trusted colleague or mentor.

✅ 4. Be ready to explain *why*

One of the easiest ways to improve your strengths answers is to **follow up with a reason**.

✅ Do:
"I enjoy bringing structure to projects — I find it satisfying to take something unclear and turn it into a step-by-step plan that others can follow."

🚫 Don't:
"My strengths are communication and time management."
(That sounds like a skills list — and gives no insight into who you are or how you think.)

📌 Final Tip:
If you're ever unsure what to say, come back to these three ingredients:

1. A strength you genuinely believe applies to you
2. A short explanation of why or how it helps you in work
3. A positive tone — but no need to brag or oversell

🎓 How Interviews Differ by Grade

One of the most common mistakes applicants make is using the **same tone, examples, and level of detail** at every grade.

The Civil Service may use the same behaviours across different roles — but the **expectations increase** significantly as you move from **EO to HEO to SEO**.

That means a great EO answer might not be good enough for an HEO role — and an HEO example could fall flat at SEO if it doesn't show enough scope, strategy, or leadership.

What Changes as You Go Up?

Let's break it down:

GRADE	WHAT THEY EXPECT	WHAT YOU NEED TO SHOW
EO	Can you follow process and deliver reliably?	Reliability, attention to detail, working well with others
HEO	Can you manage competing tasks and support wider delivery?	Independence, ownership, prioritisation, problem-solving
SEO	Can you lead, influence and deliver across teams or stakeholders?	Strategic thinking, judgement, leadership, managing risk

What This Means in Your Answers

Your STAR examples should **match the scope and impact expected at the grade**:

- **EO**: It's okay to talk about working under guidance, following set processes, or contributing to a shared task — as long as your part is clear.
- **HEO**: You should show that you can **own a piece of work**, deal with complexity, juggle priorities, and work with limited supervision.
- **SEO**: You need to show **leadership in action** — even if you didn't have formal line management. That might include influencing others, making decisions with broader impact, or improving strategic outcomes.

Tip: Think about your example and ask:

"Would someone at this grade be expected to do that — or to do more?"

If your example sounds like something a junior colleague could do, it may not score well at HEO or SEO level — even if it's a solid story.

Summary:

As the grade increases, focus your answers more on:

- Scope and ownership
- Influence and judgement
- Complexity and outcomes

The panel will be listening for signs that you can **operate confidently at the level you're applying for** — not just that you've done good work in the past.

🏛 Final Interview Tips

Even if you've never had a Civil Service interview before, there's a lot you can do to **improve your confidence and performance**. These are practical, tested tips that apply whether you're applying for EO, HEO, or SEO — and whether your interview is virtual or in person.

✅ Practice Out Loud — Not Just in Your Head

Reading your notes silently *feels* productive, but it's not enough.

You need to **speak your answers out loud**:

- It helps you find clearer ways to explain yourself
- You'll catch any awkward phrasing or areas where you ramble
- You'll improve your timing and pacing

🎙 *Bonus tip:* Record yourself answering questions and listen back. You'll hear what the panel hears — and you'll notice what to tweak.

✅ Use Notes if Allowed (Especially for Virtual Interviews)

For virtual interviews (e.g. via Microsoft Teams), most departments allow you to have **bullet points or prompt cards** nearby.

💬 *Just don't read a script word-for-word* — it sounds robotic and unnatural. Instead, have:

- A short summary for each STAR example
- A few key phrases for strengths questions
- Questions to ask the panel at the end

✅ Prepare a Behaviour Example for Every Behaviour — Plus a Spare

Even if the advert only lists three behaviours, prepare a fourth example just in case:

- You may get a follow-up question
- You may be asked about a slightly different behaviour
- You'll feel more relaxed knowing you have backups

✅ Rehearse Strengths Answers — But Don't Memorise

You can't predict which strengths questions you'll get, but you *can* practice talking naturally about your preferences.

💡 Focus on *why* something suits you — not just *what* you like.

✅ Ask the Panel a Question at the End

Most interviews end with:

"Do you have any questions for us?"

Always have one or two ready. This shows interest, initiative, and enthusiasm.

Good examples:

- "What does a successful first 3 months look like in this role?"
- "How does the team measure success or impact?"
- "What do you enjoy most about working in this department?"

✅ It's Okay to Pause Before Answering

The panel won't penalise you for taking a breath to gather your thoughts.

In fact, **a short pause and a clear answer is far better** than jumping in and rambling. You can even say:

"Let me take a second to think about the best example for that."

They'll appreciate it.

🧠 Final reminder:

You don't need to be perfect. You just need to be clear, relevant, and prepared.

📝 Example Interview Questions to Practice

Now that you know what to expect and how to prepare, the best thing you can do is **practice answering questions out loud** — just like you'll do in the interview.

Here are some realistic practice questions for both **behaviours** and **strengths**, based on real Civil Service interviews at EO, HEO, and SEO levels.

🗣 Behaviour Questions (Use STAR for Each)

These are designed to assess how you've demonstrated key Civil Service behaviours in the past.

🎯 Aim for 3–4 minutes per answer. Focus on Action and Result.

- **"Tell us about a time you improved a process."** *(Delivering at Pace)*
- **"Describe a situation where you worked with others to overcome a challenge."** *(Working Together)*
- **"Give an example of a time you had to influence someone to achieve an outcome."** *(Communicating and Influencing)*
- **"Tell us about a time you made a difficult decision and what you considered."** *(Making Effective Decisions)*
- **"Describe a time you managed competing priorities."** *(Managing a Quality Service)*

💬 Tip: Practice a mix of examples across different settings (work, volunteering, studies) to stay flexible.

Strengths Questions (Short, Authentic, and Positive)

These questions are about your **natural working style** — there are no right or wrong answers, but they should feel genuine and confident.

🎯 Keep your answers to around 1–2 minutes.

- **"What motivates you in a team setting?"**
- **"Do you enjoy working with data or people more — and why?"**
- **"How do you stay organised when managing multiple tasks?"**
- **"What does a good day at work look like for you?"**
- **"How do you approach change or uncertainty?"**

✅ Tip: Always follow up your answer with a brief "why." It adds depth and shows self-awareness.

📌 Final Note:

Don't worry if your first few practice runs feel clunky — that's completely normal. Every time you say your answers out loud, you'll get sharper and more confident.

⚠ Chapter 8: Common Mistakes & Easy Fixes

Even strong candidates get rejected — not for lack of talent, but because of small, avoidable mistakes.

Let's break down what goes wrong at each stage of the process, *why* it happens, and how you can avoid it.

🔍 At the Sift Stage

✗ 1. Not Following STAR Format

"In my role I was responsible for handling complaints, working under pressure and meeting deadlines."

This is just a list. It doesn't show what *you actually did*.

✅ **Fix:** Use STAR to walk the panel through a real-life situation — it shows your thought process, actions, and the result.

💬 **Why it matters:** Panels can't *guess* what you're capable of — they need clear evidence, or they won't award marks.

✗ 2. Too Vague or Generic

"I work well with others and always meet my deadlines."

That could be true — but it could apply to anyone.

✅ **Fix:** Add real details. What was the task? Who did you work with? What changed because of you?

💬 **Why it matters:** Specifics prove competence. Generic statements just show awareness — and that won't pass the sift.

✗ 3. Not Matching the Grade Level

Using an EO-level example in an SEO application.

✅ **Fix:** Use our behaviour comparisons to make sure your examples reflect the scope, influence, and responsibility expected at the grade.

💬 **Why it matters:** Grade fit is one of the most important things panels assess — you can do the right thing, but still get marked down if it's not the *right level* of challenge or ownership.

✖ 4. Repetition or Wasted Space

Repeating the same achievement in multiple answers.

✅ **Fix:** Use each part of the application to show something new.

💬 **Why it matters:** Panels want a well-rounded view of you. Repetition suggests you don't have a variety of relevant experience — even if you do.

✖ 5. Including Personal Information

"I studied Business at the University of Glasgow."

✅ **Fix:** Remove names of schools, cities, organisations, or anything personally identifiable.

💬 **Why it matters:** The Civil Service uses anonymous recruitment to reduce bias. Including personal info can get your application rejected without being read.

🎤 At the Interview Stage

✖ 1. Rambling Answers Without Structure

"Then we sort of changed the plan... and I guess it worked out?"

✅ **Fix:** Use STAR — keep it tight, focused, and clear.

💬 **Why it matters:** Interview panels are scoring live. If your answer is unclear or off-track, they won't award marks — even if you did a great job in real life.

✖ 2. Reciting a Script for Strengths

"My strengths are teamwork, communication, and attention to detail."

✅ **Fix:** Talk naturally about what energises you and why you enjoy it.

💬 **Why it matters:** Strengths questions are about authenticity. Scripted answers often sound forced or artificial — and panels pick up on that quickly.

❌ 3. Panicking Over Pauses

Feeling the need to speak instantly and filling time with waffle.

☑ **Fix:** Pause, breathe, and then start confidently.

💬 **Why it matters:** A short pause shows composure. A rushed answer suggests nerves or lack of clarity.

❌ 4. Saying "No" When Asked If You Have Questions

"No, I think I'm all good."

☑ **Fix:** Always ask something thoughtful. For example:

- "What's the current team priority over the next few months?"
- "What does success look like in this role after six months?"

💬 **Why it matters:** Asking a question shows genuine interest and that you've thought about the role. Saying nothing can come across as passive, unprepared, or lacking curiosity.

❌ 5. Going Off Topic

Talking about unrelated achievements that don't match the behaviour being tested.

☑ **Fix:** Re-read the question, stay focused, and bring it back to the role's responsibilities.

💬 **Why it matters:** Panels are scoring *specific* behaviours. A brilliant but unrelated story can still score zero if it doesn't answer the question.

☑ **Final Recap: Easy Wins**

☑ Use STAR — and let the Action do the heavy lifting
☑ Keep behaviour examples specific and grade appropriate
☑ Be authentic and natural in strengths responses
☑ Prepare real questions to ask the panel
☑ Practice out loud — clarity beats perfection
☑ Focus on structure, confidence, and evidence — every time

📁 Chapter 9: Templates, Tools & Final Tips

This chapter gives you the practical resources to bring everything together — from templates to planning tools and quick-reference checklists. Whether you're applying your first **EO** job or stepping into an **SEO**-level interview, this is your **application tool**

📄 1. Behaviour Statement Planner (STAR)

Use this simple planner for each behaviour you're asked to demonstrate. Don't write the full version yet — just capture key points.

SECTION	PROMPT	NOTES
SITUATION	What was the context? Where were you working, and what was the scenario?	
TASK	What were *you* responsible for? What outcome was expected?	
ACTION	What did *you* personally do? What steps did you take? How did you adapt or lead?	
RESULT	What happened? What changed? Was there any feedback, outcome, or learning?	

🔁 Repeat for every behaviour in the job advert.

📋 2. Word Count Tracker

Keep track of your key application sections and make sure you're staying within limits:

SECTION	WORD LIMIT	WORD COUNT	STATUS
CV / EXPERIENCE BOX	250–500		☐ Draft ☐ Final
PERSONAL STATEMENT	500–1,250		☐ Draft ☐ Final
BEHAVIOUR 1	250		☐ Draft ☐ Final
BEHAVIOUR 2	250		☐ Draft ☐ Final
BEHAVIOUR 3	250		☐ Draft ☐ Final

📌 Tip: Aim for 85–95% of the word limit — enough to show depth, but not filler.

🧠 3. Civil Service Buzzword Bank (to Reflect Role Language)

Use the job advert as your guide — but these phrases commonly appear in high-scoring applications:

- Worked collaboratively across teams
- Adapted my approach to suit the audience
- Took ownership of the process
- Escalated risks where appropriate
- Improved efficiency by streamlining X
- Ensured compliance with internal guidance
- Handled sensitive information with discretion
- Used evidence to support decision-making
- Delivered under tight deadlines

☑ Use these phrases **authentically**, only where they reflect your real experience.

4. Self-Checklist Before You Submit

Use this quick checklist before hitting submit:

- ☑ CV section tailored to the job advert
- ☑ Personal statement is anonymised and focused
- ☑ Each behaviour answer follows STAR
- ☑ Actions and outcomes are clearly shown
- ☑ Examples are at the right grade
- ☑ You've proofread your application for clarity and flow
- ☑ You've prepared for strengths AND behaviour interview questions
- ☑ You've prepared questions to ask the panel
- ☑ You know how to access your application portal again

💬 **Top Tip: Keep a copy of everything you submit — you'll need it to prep for your interview!**

5. Prompt Ideas for Using AI Tools (Like ChatGPT)

AI can help you draft, edit, or refine — but it works best when you give it clear instructions.

Here are examples of what to ask:

- "Can you help me write a 250-word STAR example for 'Working Together' at **HEO** level?"
- "Rewrite this paragraph to make it sound more confident and concise."

- "Give me five realistic strength-based interview questions for an **EO** caseworker role."
- "Check this behaviour example for clarity and flow — does it show impact?"

⚠ **Reminder: Always check and personalise anything AI tools help you write. Your application must sound like *you* — not a robot.**

🌟 Final Thought

By now, you've seen how to:

☑ Understand Civil Service roles and grades

☑ Write a tailored CV and personal statement

☑ Nail behaviour statements with STAR

☑ Avoid common mistakes

☑ Prepare confidently for interview

You've got the tools — now it's time to take the next step.

Whether this is your first application or your fiftieth, you're better equipped than most people applying. And if you keep applying what you've learned here, **your offer will come**.

So give yourself credit. Keep going. And when the email lands with *"We're pleased to invite you to interview..."* — you'll be ready.

🎓 Chapter 10: Final Words: Good Luck — What Awaits You

Congratulations for making it this far — not just in reading this book, but in taking the next step towards a meaningful and stable career.

Applying for Civil Service roles can be intense, competitive, and at times frustrating. But the rewards — both personal and professional — are worth the effort. Whether this is your first attempt or your fifth, I want to leave you with some encouragement and a glimpse of what makes this career path so worthwhile.

📷 Why the Civil Service?

From my own experience, here are just a few of the real, everyday benefits of working in the Civil Service:

📊 1. Professional Development

There are constant opportunities to grow. Whether through mentoring, on-the-job learning, or formal qualifications (often funded), your development is taken seriously. The Civil Service invests in its people — not just in theory, but in practice.

🛡 2. Job Security

In an uncertain world, this matters more than ever. The Civil Service offers genuine long-term stability. It's not about coasting — it's about building a future where your work, your income, and your growth aren't constantly under threat.

🏛 3. Recognised, Respected Work

Whether you're processing applications, managing funding, or supporting frontline delivery, you're part of a recognised and respected national structure. Civil Service experience is highly transferable and valued across sectors.

✦ 4. Structure and Clarity

There's comfort and confidence in knowing what's expected of you. Roles are clearly defined, promotion routes are visible, and guidance is available. You're not left to guess how to succeed — the frameworks are there to help you.

5. A Strong Pension and Fair Benefits

The Civil Service offers one of the best pension schemes in the UK. Annual leave, parental leave, and flexible working options are generous. You're not just doing meaningful work — you're looked after while doing it.

---

6. Impact That Matters

You might be one cog in a big machine, but what you do affects real lives. Whether you're helping individuals access services, improving policy, or enabling vital infrastructure — your work counts.

One Last Piece of Advice

You don't need to be perfect. You just need to be clear, committed, and able to show what you bring to the table.

Use this guide. Use your own voice. And most of all — **keep going**.

You've got this.

Wishing you the very best of luck — and hoping to see you in the Civil Service soon.

🙏 Acknowledgements

Writing this guide has been both a professional project and a personal reflection on the journey into the Civil Service.

Thank you to **Scott and Frances**, my mum and dad, for your continual support throughout my life — every step of the way, all the way into the Civil Service and beyond. Your encouragement has meant more than words can say.

To everyone who shared their stories, frustrations, and advice along the way — thank you. This book is shaped by real experiences, and it's written for every person trying to navigate this process with honesty, confidence, and ambition.

Printed in Dunstable, United Kingdom